The non-royal regular feminine titles of the Middle Kingdom and Second Intermediate Period: Dossiers

Danijela Stefanović

Golden House Publications

London 2009

This title is published by
Golden House Publications

Cover Image: Unterside of a scarab found at Naqada; UC 11353 © University College London

Printed in the United Kingdom, by

Antony Rowe Limited
CPI Group

ISBN 978-1-906137-12-0

Acknowledgment

I would like to thank Prof. Dr. Helmut Satzinger, Dr. Vera Vasiljević and Dr. Wolfram Grajetzki for all their help and support. My acknowledgments go likewise to Dr. Stephen Quirke and Dr. Katalin Anna Kóthay for sending me offprints of their articles. For the cover picture, I am grateful to Dr. Stephen Quirke (Petrie Museum of Egyptian Archaeology / UCL Institute of Archaeology). However, any errors and inconsistencies are entirely my own.

INTRODUCTION

In the historiography of ancient societies (including the Egyptian) there has appeared, since the 1960s, a great number of works relevant to the study of women in antiquity.[1] At present there are several studies presenting a "comprehensive social model"[2] and general surveys for the Egyptian woman,[3] many of them being influenced by S. Pomeroy's *Goddesses, Whores, Wives, and Slaves* (New York 1979) and P. W. Pestman's study of marriage and the legal position of women.[4] Along with more general overviews, the focus of attention has also been on particular aspects of the role of woman in society,[5] particular 'professions',[6] female literacy,[7] social

---

[1] See Rawson, in: *Women in antiquity*, 1-20.

[2] Noblecourt, *La femme au temps des pharaons*; Millard, *The Position of Women in the Family and in Society*; Robins, *Women in Ancient Egypt*; Pomeroy, *Women in Hellenistic Egypt*; Montserrat, *Sex and Society in Graeco-Roman Egypt*; O'Brien, *Egyptian Women in Ptolemaic and Roman Egypt*; O'Brien, *Women in Demotic Business and Administrative Texts*; Johnson, in: *The Life of Meresamun*, 82-91.

[3] Tyldesley, *Daughters of Isis*; Watterson, *Women in Ancient Egypt*. See also Wilfong, *Women in Ancient Near East*.

[4] Pestman, *Marriage and Matrimonial Property*.

[5] Millard, *Position of Women in the Family and in Society*; Robins, *Women in Ancient Egypt*; Lesko, *Women's earliest records*; Johnson, in: *Mistress of the House, Mistress of Heaven,* 175-86 and 215-18; Szpakowska, *Daily Life in Ancient Egypt*.

[6] Onstine, *The Role of the Chantress (šmyt)*; Gillam, *JARCE* 32, 1995, 211-237; Roehrig, *Royal nurse*; Eyre, in: *Le commerce en Égypte ancienne*, 173-192; Roehrig, in: *Mistress of the House, Mistress of Heaven*, 14-27; Lorenz, in: *The Life of Meresamun*, 98-101.

[7] Sweeney, in: *Sesto Congresso Internazionale di Egittologia*, 523-529; Lesko, in: *Studies Wente*, 247-254; Baines, *Visual and written*, 63-94; Grajetzki, Women and writing in the Middle Kingdom: Stela Louvre C 187 (in preparation).

groups,[8] and specific places.[9] However, it was mainly queens and elite women[10] that received substantial attention because the non-elite women (especially those of low economic and social status) are, according to the general opinion, underrepresented in historical sources. As J. Baines observes, *most women of the highest status had no administrative position. The men in the same circles all had official posts, whether or not such posts involved real work; in theory they had an occupation and the women did not.*[11]

The theoretical issues of gender construction[12] and differentiation have been investigated in the context of archaeological data from individual sites,[13] as well as in respect to language.[14] Queer theory has also begun to form an area of investigation for Egyptologists.[15] Still, there are very few studies that cover women in specific historical periods.[16] The life of an Egyptian woman, including the analysis of various feminine titles, a woman's role as a member of a household, and her economic and legal activity, whether on behalf of

---

[8] Kóthay, *Acta Antiqua Academiae Scientiarum Hungaricae* 46, 2006, 151-164; Hofmann, *bȝk* und *ḥm*; Id., in: *Living and Writing in Deir el-Medina*, 113-118.

[9] For example Toivari-Viitali, *Women at Deir el-Meina*; Sweeney, in: *Living and Writing in Deir el-Medina*, 135-153; Quirke, in: *Archaeology and Women*, 246-262.

[10] For a discussion of elite women and their titles in the Late Period, see Johnson, in: *Studies Quaegebeur* 1393-1421; cf. Lorenz, in: *The Life of Meresamun*, 98; Graefe, *Gottesgemahlin des Amun*.

[11] Baines, *Visual and written*, 88.

[12] For a general overview see Roth, in: *A Companion to the Ancient Near East*, 227-234 and, especially for the Middle Kingdom, Lustig, in: *Anthropology and Egyptology*, 43-65.

[13] Meskell, *Archaeologies of Social Life.* See a general overview by C. Graves-Brown, in: *Sex and Gender in Ancient Egypt*, ix-xxv.

[14] Sweney, in: *Sex and Gender in Ancient Egypt*, 191-214, with extensive bibliography.

[15] Parkinson, *JEA* 81, 1995, 57-76; Parkinson, in: *Sex and Gender in Ancient Egypt*, 115-142.

[16] See, for example, Fischer, *Egyptian Women*; various contributions in Lesko, *Women's earliest records*; Pomeroy, *Women in Hellenistic Egypt*, etc.

her family or in her own right, and how these differed from or were the same as those of an Egyptian man, have also been studied.[17]

The present knowledge of the feminine titles of the Middle Kingdom and Second Intermediate Period is based upon the works of A. M. Blackman (his study "On the position of women in the ancient Egyptian hierarchy", *JEA* 7, 1921, 8-30, is one of the earliest to deal with a number of women's titles), E. M. Guest (Women's Titles in the Middle Kingdom, *Ancient Egypt*, June 1926, 46-50), A. Millard (*The Position of Women in the Family and in Society in Ancient Egypt: with special reference to the Middle Kingdom.* 3 vols. London: University of London 1976 [unpublished]), W. Ward (*Essays on Feminine Titles of the Middle Kingdom and Related Subjects*, Beirut 1986, and Non-royal Women and their Occupations in the Middle Kingdom, in: *Women's Earliest Records: From Ancient Egypt and Western Asia*, ed. by B. Lesko, Atlanta 1989, 33-43), H. G. Fischer (*Egyptian Women of the Old Kingdom and of the Heracleopolitan Period,* New York 1989), as well as on the various studies of G. Robins, O. D. Berlev, D. Franke, W. Grajetzki, and S. Quirke, dealing with titles and Middle Kingdom society in a wider sense. All mentioned authors have worked intensively with prosopographical data, reconstructing genealogies and careers of important functionaries (basically male), and only some of them were dealing with the female title-holders also.

The work of W. Ward is of special importance. He manages to distinguish three groups of feminine title-holders in respect of the rank and social status of their husbands.[18] The women from the first group were wives of high-ranking officials of the central and provincial administration. The wives of minor officials belong to the

---

[17] See, for example, valuable contributions of A. K. Capel and G. E. Markoe (*Mistress of the House, Mistress of Heaven: Women in Ancient Egypt*), A. O'Brien (*Women in Demotic Business and Administrative Texts*), and most recently E. Teeter and J. H. Johnson (*The Life of Meresamun*) with further bibliography.

[18] Ward, *Feminine Titles*, 24-28; compare with Fischer, *Egyptian Studies* I, 76-79, and Millard, *Position of Women in the Family and in Society*, 259-345.

second group. Titles from the third group basically refer to the household servants and attendants.

The Middle Kingdom feminine titles have been divided, by D. Franke, into three main categories covering 49 different areas of female activity:[19]

I Female household attendants (so-called administrative titles; titles of the women working for private households, royal courts or temples; it is possible to classify under this entry about 27 different professions);

II Religious titles and music - priestess, dancers, singers, i.e. all titles dealing with the cultic practice;

III Rank titles - designations of social status of non-royal women.

In comparison with the Old Kingdom, there is a significant decline of the number of feminine titles, as well as of title-holders.[20] H. G. Fischer pointed out that *it is difficult to avoid the impression that women of the Middle Kingdom were less frequently and significantly engaged in administering people and property than was previously the case – not that their role was ever of great importance except, of course, in the case of mother, wife, or daughter of the king.*[21] The offices of treasurer,[22] messenger, chief steward and mayor, professions of artisanship (draftspersons, sculptors, carpenters, or coppersmiths, employed by either the state or the temples) or various construction works have seldom, if ever, been attested for Middle Kingdom women.

While women appear rarely in the trades and professions, we find them as hairdressers, cosmeticians, brewers, millers, weavers, and

---

[19] Franke, *JEA* 76, 1990, 228.

[20] B. M. Bryan maintains that there is a great difference in preserved sources, competing the Old and Middle Kingdom as far more tomb inscriptions are available from the Old Kingdom than later, and on the other hand, the Middle Kingdom data basically derive from the votive stelae on which female servants and household members are recorded (Bryan, in: *Mistress of the House, Mistress of Heaven*, 39).

[21] Fischer, *Egyptian Studies* I, 79.

[22] See Ward, *Feminine Titles*, 36-37. Women's administrative titles in general, and especially during the Late period, belong to the service of women for women.

gardeners, and many of them worked in large private households.[23] Furthermore, Middle Kingdom women were often conscripted as part of government corveés for the large work projects or employed in linen manufacture, as is shown, for example, in the weaving scene found in the tomb of Khnumhotep at Beni Hasan - five women, of all ages, are shown engaged in various stages of linen manufacture.[24]

The role of Egyptian women in the production of textiles is attested as early as the Old Kingdom.[25] G. Robins notes, in respect of scenes and models representing textile production on large estates, that *these women are probably servants rather than members of the household estate.*[26] The letter of *nbt-pr ỉrr* (London, UC 32203)[27] records that she was entrusted with women who are unable to weave. Their unefficientness caused that *ỉrr* could not deliver the amount of woven linen expected from her. Irer informed her superior that she was occupied with her duties in the temple. The weavers, subordinated to her, were "left abandoned, thinking they wouldn't get food provisions inasmuch as not any news of you has been heard". She stresses that her superior "should spend some time here since [not] any clothes [have been made] while my attention is being directed to the temple, and the warp-threads are set up on the loom without it being possible to weave them".[28] Furthermore, one of the Hekanakhte letters records an arrangement with women about the processing of his flax harvest, while a late Middle Kingdom papyrus lists twenty women who are designated as cloth-makers.[29] On the

---

[23] See: Millard, *Position of Women in the Family and in Society*, 259-345.

[24] Newberry, *Beni Hasan* I, pl. XXIX; *Beni Hasan* II, pl. IV; Klebs, *Reliefs*, 125-127.

[25] See: Szpakowska, *Daily Life in Ancient Egypt*, 81-90.

[26] Robins, *Women in Ancient Egypt*, 103. See also, Lorenz, in: *The Life of Meresamun*, 99 and Roehrig, in: *Mistress of the House, Mistress of Heaven*, 13.

[27] Collier-Quirke, *The UCL Lahun Papyri: Letters*, 115-118; Quirke, in: *Archaeology and Women*, 251.

[28] Wente, *Letters*, 82-83. See Quirke, in: *Archaeology and Women*, 251 and Lorenz, in: *The Life of Meresamun*, 99-100.

[29] Hayes, *Papyrus Brooklyn*, 105-107; Берлев, *Трудовое население*, 17-22; Roehrig, in: *Mistress of the House, Mistress of Heaven*, 21; cf. Quirke, in: *Archaeology and Women*, 251.

other hand, in respect to the food preparation, or various agricultural activities, Middle Kingdom titles are almost completely male.[30]

This does not mean, however, that during the Middle Kingdom women could not take an active role in economy nor that they were denied economic independence.[31] While they are not generally found in public life, especially during the Middle Kingdom,[32] this does not mean that careers for individual women were impossible, although administration and the professions were, as a rule, not areas in which women played a role. From the Middle Kingdom there are a few cases of the feminine *sš* . These have been discussed by Fischer,[33] who concludes that at least one example on a scarab should mean that its owner was a 'female scribe'. On the other hand, W. Grajetzki convincingly argues that the meaning of the title *sšt* rather points to 'cosmetician'.[34]

However, titles referring to the female household attendants (dealing with so-called administrative titles), titles of the women working for private households, royal courts or temples, and titles dealing with the cultic practice (titles connected with cult and music, i.e. priestess, dancers, singers, etc)[35] suggest that 'careers' for individual women were possible.

Female *wʿb*-priestesses are attested on Middle Kingdom monuments.[36] For example, one inscription addresses male and female *ḥmt-nṯr* priests, *wʿb* priests, and chanters and chantresses (*ḫnwt*) of the temple.[37] There are records of female priestesses in the

---

[30] See Ward, *Index MK*; Quirke, in: *Archaeology and Women*, 252.

[31] See especially various contributions in Lesko, *Women's earliest records*; Roehrig, in: *Mistress of the House, Mistress of Heaven*, Robins, *Women in Ancient Egypt*, 127-141, and Millard, *Position of Women in the Family and in Society*, 345-359.

[32] See Quirke, in: *Studies in Honour of H. S. Smith,* 227-235; Ward, in: *Women's Earliest Records*, 33-43; Onstine, *The Role of the Chantress (šmyt)*.

[33] Fischer, *Egyptian Studies* I, 73, 77–78.

[34] W. Grajetzki, Women and writing in the Middle Kingdom: Stela Louvre C 187 (in preparation).

[35] Franke, *JEA* 76, 1990, 228.

[36] Ward, *Index MK*, 690-692; Quirke, *Titles and bureaux*, 124.

[37] Sethe, *Ägyptische Lesestücke*, 87 (lines 21-22).

temples at Abydos and Beni Hasan, as well as in the cult of Hathor during the Early Middle Kingdom. R. Gillam observes that the disappearance of *ḥmwt-nṯr ḥtḥr* from the cultic practice of the Middle Kingdom is one of the best examples of the process of decline of women's role in the public life.[38] It is important to note that along with the decline of the title *ḥmt-nṯr ḥtḥr*, some other regular feminine titles also vanished from the sources by the reign of Senwosret II: the *ẖkrt-nswt wꜤtt*, *Ꜥḥ Ꜥyt* and *ẖtt-pr*. It may easily be that the recognised features have nothing in common (high ranking / low ranking titles; administrative / rank titles) but disappearance of the titles belongs to the same chronological framework. Women with the priestly title "God's Wife" are also attested for the cults of Min, Amun, Ptah and other deities in the Middle Kingdom.

However, one of the main problems in respect of the studies of the feminine titles is that the majority of them do not appear in any conclusive context and many of them cannot be understood with accuracy. Since their meanings and functions are often unknown, the duties and the rank of an individual can rarely be determined. In this respect, the title *nbt-pr,* the commonest feminine title of the Middle Kingdom, and the dynastic period as a whole, is perhaps the best example.[39]

There is a general opinion that the scope of activities of nebet per, according to K. Szpakowska's translation 'lady of estate',[40] would have included the important duties of administering large households with scores of servants, workshops for weaving, preparing food supplies, making clothes, and fruit and vegetable gardens. Szpakowska points out that the nebet per, the most common feminine title of the Middle Kingdom, seems to be associated, as also some other titles, with married women 'whose husbands held higher rank'. Acquisition of the title was perhaps based on their husband's rank.[41]

---

[38] Gillam, *JARCE* 32, 1995, 214, 233-234.

[39] See Fischer, *Egyptian Studies* I, 76, n. 46; Millard, *Position of Women in the Family and in Society*, 262.

[40] Szpakowska, *Daily Life in Ancient Egypt*, 109.

[41] Szpakowska, *Daily Life in Ancient Egypt*, 109.

According to A. Millard *the overt meaning of nbt pr is that the bearer is the female head of a household, and, in normal circumstances, she would be the wife of the man of the house.*[42] She also stresses that *nbt pr* may be a synonym for wife *but it would only be of those whose wealth was such that they had a household of several people to manage.*[43]

W. Ward assumes that the 'ubiquitous' title *nbt-pr, claimed by women of all stations*, indicate *the wife's duties as director of households affairs.*[44] The 'lady of the house' was therefore often in charge of a substantial community and it was her job to see that it functioned effectively.[45] For J. Toivari-Viitala, the title *nbt-pr* is perhaps an indication that the woman was at the head of the household, regardless of whether she had a husband.[46] D. Franke maintains that the title belonged to the legal wife only.[47] J. H. Johnson suggests that title was used to indicate married women. The term may not only point to the women's role in charge of the house, but also indicate that she owned her own property.[48]

However, it is important to note that, according to the almost five hundred Middle Kingdom attestations (most of them from the Late Middle Kingdom)[49] of the title in question (collected by D. Stefanović), almost 80% were of a very modest background[50] and less then 60% were married (see, for example, Bolton 10.20, with six

---

[42] Millard, *Position of Women in the Family and in Society*, 264, cf. 265-266, 304-304.

[43] Millard, *Position of Women in the Family and in Society*, 305.

[44] Ward, *Feminine Titles*, 24, 8.

[45] Szpakowska, *Daily Life in Ancient Egypt*, 109. Cf. Ward, in: *Women's Earliest Records*, 33-43.

[46] Toivari-Viitala, *Women at Deir el-Medina*, 15-18; cf. Robins, *Women in Ancient Egypt*, 92.

[47] Franke, *AVB*, 38-9.

[48] She also notes the large number of women from the Late Period who are recorded on their funerary stelae bearing the title *nbt-pr* together with a title as musician. Johnson, in: *The Life of Meresamun*, 86, n. 18. See also Johnson, in: *Studies Quaegebeur* 1393-1421.

[49] According to the J. Garstang list of titles, almost 30 *nbt-pr* were buried in the lower necropolis of Beni Hasan (Garstang, *Burial Customs*, vii-viii).

[50] Cf. Orel, in: *Studies Share*, 236.

nbt-pr recorded on the family stela, and Saffron Walden Museum 1892.49 with twelve *nbt-pr*).

My aim in this study is to outline what we know of the various regular non-royal feminine titles (i.e. those which appear in non-royal usage) and their functions during the Middle Kingdom and Second Intermediate Period, and then to look briefly at the careers of some of their holders. First of all, to show that the non-elite women, with their names and titles, are well attested in the sources, and that it is possible to create dossiers for these women.

However, any research on titles must be linked to prosopographic work and kinship studies. This study is thus based on two elements: the compilation of a database, i.e. a compilation of dossiers of the 'regular non-royal feminine title-holders', and in-depth analyses of the titles held by these women. Each dossier will list all the records that are of relevance for the person described, the data that refers to family members and the references to the person in prosopographic studies that already exist. Within each unit the data would be grouped in the same manner: *Name of title-holder, Lists of the records in which the title bearer is attested, Records in which other titles are attested, Data on the members of immediate and wider family*. If all the available relevant information on each individual could be put into a standardised format and collected in a single database, it would be a simple task to do very comprehensive analyses upon them.

The dossiers has been sorted to create groups of individuals who share the same characteristics: I *iryt-pꜥt,* II *ꜥnḫt nt niwt,* III *ꜥnḫt nt nswt tpt,* IV *ꜥḫꜥyt,* V *ꜥḳyt,* VI *wbꜣyt,* VII *bꜣḳt nt ḥḳꜣ,* VIII *mnꜥt,* IX *ḥsyt,* X *ḫtt-pr*, and XI *ẖkrt-nswt*. Why these titles? First, all of them belong to the group of regular[51] Middle Kingdom and Second Intermediate Period feminine titles (i.e. there are more than five attestations) with the limited number of title-holders (i.e. no more than 150). Of course, it would be hard to think that the lists of attestations are definitive, but in the moment, they provide us with a very solid amount of information. Second, different social groups are attested among title-holders sometimes even within the same group.

---

[51] Cf. Quirke, *RdÉ*, 37, 1986, 107.

On this basis, careers and functions (if there are any) of the individuals are reconstructed as exactly as possible.

The data on the members of women's immediate and wider families are of great importance. Because women seldom had their own tombs or stelae,[52] the monuments of their fathers, husbands, and sons provide most genealogical data. The titles held by these men, and in some cases by female relatives, are indication of their social standing as the status and self-identity spread from the man to his wife,[53] and sometimes vice-versa.

Furthermore, the dossiers contribute to determining whether or not one title was inherited or otherwise influenced by a family's affiliations. Since professions and jobs were frequently handed down through families, male or female kin were also part of their identity. The most commonly examined Middle Kingdom and Second Intermediate Period non-royal feminine titles in this respect are *ḥmt-nṯr ḥtḥr*[54] and *šmꜥyt*.[55] By breaking down the data into relationships (mother / daughter; father / daughter; mother-in-law / daughter-in-law; husband / wife) and comparing the level of similarity between the titles of the two individuals, it is possible to speculate about factors that influenced a woman's decision to 'chose a certain profession'. M. Galvin's results with the priestesses of Hathor state that there was no consistent pattern to suggest the hereditary status of a Hathoric title of any family member.[56]

The issues of feminine titles can not be separated from the fields of gender and women studies, moving from a primary concern with the place of women in history to a study of the construction of gender. Since my work is committed to searching for attestations of women within the record, it would in this respect be a continuation of the first wave of feminist studies,[57] which was primarily concerned with

---

[52] Stefanović, *GM* 218, 2008, 86-90; Id., *GM* 220, 2009, 95-98.

[53] Johnson, in: *The Life of Meresamun*, 83-84.

[54] Galvin, *Priests and Priestesses of Hathor*.

[55] Onstine, *The Role of the Chantress (šmyt)*.

[56] Galvin, *Priests and Priestesses of Hathor*, 173-204; Id., *JEA* 70, 1984, 42-49.

[57] For a summary of the 'three waves' of feminism, see Meskell, *Archaeologies of Social Life*, 54-56.

locating and documenting women in the historical records. In this respect, collecting the 'database' of the feminine title-holders could perhaps be recognised as an outdated methodological approach. Whereas this is true, our presumptions and conclusions would be in a way misleading if we do not have a clear picture of how many women held a certain title, was it inherited or not within the family, was it a pre-married or post-married designation, or were they 'visible' through their names and titles, or not (written records, iconography, archaeology) while being household servants. Furthermore, the database of regular feminine title-holders is perhaps one of solutions for one of the main problems for gender approaches to ancient history, i.e. the problem of sources and their interpretation. In case of database, there is no need for 'reading between the lines' which is a good starting point for preventing the reproach that the historian is 'imposing' his / her prejudices on the sources.[58] Of course, the study of women in any society (ancient or modern) or epoch is, and must be, interdisciplinary.

The specific nature of the aforementioned titles, within the chronological frame of the Middle Kingdom and Second Intermediate Period, is investigated by dossiers that catalogue women. In this respect I am more inclined to assume that this small study is rather a contribution to social history than one to gender studies or women history.

[58] Morley, *Ancient History*, 87.

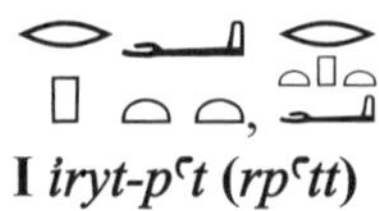

I *iryt-pꜥt* (*rpꜥtt*)

The title *iryt-pꜥt* was a permanent element in the titulary of queens from the sixth dynasty onward.[59] During the Middle Kingdom and Second Intermediate Period it also appears in non-royal usage, although it was still used by king's mothers, sisters and daughters.[60] One of the most characteristic examples of the non-royal usage of the title *iryt-pꜥt* is attested within the nomarch families of Beni Hasan.

Sat-Ipy, the wife of Beni Hasan nomach Khnumhotep I was, as W. Ward noted, one of the earliest *iryt-pꜥt*,[61] while at the same time she held the titles *ḥmt ḥḳꜣ*, *ḫnt ḥmwt nbwt* and *nbt-pr*.[62] It is however not impossible, as Ward pointed out, that she was a member of the royal family.[63] Their daughter Baqet, the wife of the *iry-pꜥt ḥꜣty-ꜥ ḥḳꜣ niwwt mꜣwwt nḫri*, was also *iryt-pꜥt* as well as *ḥꜣtyt-ꜥ*.[64] *Ḫty*, the wife of their son, the nomarch Khnumhotep II, held the titles *iryt-pꜥt ḥꜣtyt-ꜥ sꜣt-ḥꜣty-ꜥ nbt-pr rḫt-nswt ḥmt-nṯr ḥtḥr ḥmt-nṯr pꜣḫt*. She was the daughter of a *ḥḳꜣ n inpwt*.[65] Ward draws attention to the fact that *ḫty* did not belong to the royal family, but was the offspring of an important provincial family.[66]

According to Ward, it is possible that none of the Beni Hasan *iryt-pꜥt* were of royal origin. They held the title *by virtue of their high*

---

[59] Ward, *Index MK*, 857; Millard, *Position of Women in the Family and in Society*, 267-269; Jones, *Index of Ancient Egyptian Titles*, 1247; Hanning, *Ägyptisches Wörterbuch II*, 343-344; Troy, *Patterns of Queenship*, 133

[60] Troy, *Patterns of Queenship*, 133; Millard, *Position of Women in the Family and in Society*, 524. n. 14; Franke, *JEA* 76, 1990, 229.

[61] Cf. I/17.

[62] Newberry, *Beni Hasan* I, pl. 46; *Urk*. VII, 13; Ward, *Feminine Titles*, 46

[63] Ward, *Feminine Titles*, 46

[64] Newberry, *Beni Hasan* I, pl. 25; *Urk*. VII, 28. Cf. I/3.

[65] Newberry, *Beni Hasan* II, pl. 24. Cf. I/16.

[66] Ward, *Feminine titles*, 46

station as mothers and wives of nomarchs.[67] Based on examples recorded in his list of attestations, Ward concluded that *unless clear evidence exists to the contrary, the title Hereditary Noblewomen was honorific during this period* (i.e. Late Middle Kingdom).[68] His assumption is based on the fact that the masculine counterpart was a well-attested rank title without royal connotations. For Ward, the title *iryt-pꜥt* marked a woman's status within society and was perhaps adopted after marriage.[69]

Millard points out that the available data are too merge to draw any conclusion concerning the significance and rank of the title *iryt-pꜥt*, whether acquired before or after marriage, *but in the two cases where something is known about the family background of these women* (i.e. the nomarchs' families of Beni Hasan) *both can be shown to the considerable heiresses, bringing more into their husband's families than a simple dowry. It is therefore possible that iryt-pꜥt does denote heiress.*[70]

When analysing the XVII Dynasty stela of *iry-pꜥt ḥꜣty-ꜥ mr pr wr mḥb* from Tell Edfu,[71] J. Baines noted that the title *iryt-pꜥt* (in this case the title of Emhab's mother)[72] is a rare title for women, and probably, along with his titles, relates to Emhab's position as nomarch (?). His suggestion is based on the assumption that *almost all examples with non-royal women of the Middle Kingdom and Second Intermediate Period belong to wives of nomarchs and people of similar status.*[73]

The *iryt-pꜥt* kwms also needs to be noted. She is attested, with the title *iryt-pꜥt,* on the stela Paris, Louvre C 287 [E.13057][74] as the mother of a *ḥꜣty-ꜥ mr ḥwt-nṯr sꜣ-nswt ṯsw iwꜥy n ꜣbḏw* and wife of *sš*

[67] Ward, *Feminine titles*, 46; cf. Millard, *Position of Women in the Family and in Society*, 268.

[68] Ward, *Feminine titles*, 46 (54-56).

[69] Ward, *Feminine titles*, 46.

[70] Millard, *Position of Women in the Family and in Society*, 270.

[71] Cairo, JdE 49566; Baines, *JEA* 72, 1986, 41-53.

[72] Cf. I/4.

[73] Baines, *JEA* 72, 1986, 51, n. 44. Cf. I/22.

[74] Franke, *JEA* 71, 1985, 175-6 pl. xix; cf. Id, *Doss.,* 204, 712.

ḥtpw-nṯr wp-w3wt-iry.[75] Her husband is recorded, with the same title, on the stela London, BM EA 833 (+ Paris, Louvre E 6167).[76] Here also, a woman is attested with the rare name *kwms*, though with the title *ẖkrt-nswt*. If the *kwms* from London and the *kwms* from Paris are one and the same person, her title *iryt-pˁt* would speak in favour of Ward's theory. In this case, BM EA 833 may be earlier than Louvre C 287 [E.13057], since she is not termed as *ḥmt.f.* The other possibility is that *kwms* held both titles as marks of her noble origin and her social standing close to the court circle.

Another puzzling *iryt-pˁt* was *sbk-nḫt.*[77] A small copper statuette depicts a *sbk-nḫt* seated on ground and breast-feeding a small child with a side lock. J. F. Romano tried to identify her with *sbk-nḫt*, mother of prince Ibiaw, suggesting *that the child may have been a crown prince on account of the side lock.*[78] The identification does not seem likely since this Sobeknakht does not bear the title *s3t-nswt*, which was the title of Ibiaw's mother; use of the title *iryt-pˁt* would certainly not lead to the exclusion of the title *s3t-nswt* since the later expresses direct filiation to the king and is therefore explicit.[79]

However, the long inscription of Khnumhotep II provides us with one important detail. When narrating about his origin, he says about

---

[75] Franke, *Doss.*, 204.

[76] Clère, *JEA* 68, 1982, 60-68.

[77] Brooklin Museum of Fine Arts, 43.137. Cf. I/19.

[78] Romano, *MDAIK* 48, 1992, 131-143; Markoe - Capel, *Mistress of the House, Mistress of Heaven*, 60-61.

[79] Ryholt, *SIP*, 280. n. 1017. The *iryt-pˁt mr.s-tḫ* is perhaps also worth of notice. She is attested on four monuments: Petrie, *Season*, nos 175 and 176, Habachi, *Elephantine* IV, no 16 and Boston MFA 71.403. On the first two monuments *mr.s-tḫ* is recorded without titles, as mother of the *wḥmw ˁnḫw*. At some point she has become *snt-nswt* and *iryt-pˁt* (Habachi, *Elephantine* IV, no 16 and Boston MFA 71.403), while her son was awarded the post of the overseer of fields and highest rank titles (cf. Franke, *Doss.*, 177, Id., *Miscellanea Aegyptologica*, 67-87, and Grajetzki, *Zentralverwaltung*, 131-132). It is possible that *mr.s-tḫ* acquired her rank title *iryt-pˁt* as king's sister; i.e. the title was not a mark of her noble origin by birth but rather the sign of a newly established 'conection' with the king's house (I am grateful to W. Grajetzki who has kindly drawn my attention to the person of *mr.s-tḫ*).

his mother: … *wḏ3 mwt.i r iryt-pʿt ḥ3tyt-ʿ m s3t ḥḳ3 n m3-ḥḏ* "… my mother having gone to be *iryt-pʿt* (and) *ḥ3tyt-ʿ* as the daughter of the ruler of the Oryx nome." Thus, *b3kt* has been described as becoming *iryt-pʿt* and *ḥ3tyt-ʿ* as the daughter of the ruler of the Oryx nome, and the wife of *iry-pʿt ḥ3ty-ʿ ḥḳ3 niwwt m3wwt nḥri.*[80] It seems that Khnumhotep's mother did not become *iryt-pʿt* as the wife of a nomarch, but rather as being a lady of noble origin, and thus an appropriate wife for *nḥri*.

It is possible that *iryt-pʿt*, in both royal and non-royal usage, was a feminine rank title, the mark of a woman's noble origin (royal, court circle, provincial nobility), and was not necessarily connected with her marital status, i.e. not necessarily a sign of a social standing inherited from husband.[81] Their noble origin perhaps made of them suitable consorts for high-ranking officials.

I/1 ***3st*** [3/18][82]

Cairo, JdE 42201 (Daressy, *ASAE* 17, 1917, 240-241).

Husband	*ḥ3ty-ʿ mr ḥmw-nṯr ib-iʿw*
Daughter	*nbt-pr s3t-ḥr*
Son-in-law	*ḥry-ḥb n ḥr bḥdt*

I/2 ***ʿtt*** [72/5]

Cairo, JdE 75174 (Martin, *Seals*, 386).

I/3 ***b3kt*** [90/12]

Beni Hasan, Tomb 3 (Newberry, *Beni Hasan* I, pl. 25).

**ḥ3tyt-ʿ*

Husband	*iry-pʿt ḥ3ty-ʿ ḥḳ3 niwwt m3wwt nḥri*

---

[80] See: Newberry, *Beni Hasan* I, pl. XXV, lines 62-68; Breasted, *Ancient Records of Egypt* I, §628; B. Bryan, in: *Misters of the House*, 37; Troy, *Patterns of Queenship*, 133.

[81] Cf. Tyldesley, *Daughters of Isis*, 121; Szpakowska, *Daily Life in Ancient Egypt*; 109 Robins, *Women in Ancient Egypt*, 115.

[82] See: Ward, *Feminine Titles*, 54/3, and Millard, *Position of Women in the Family and in Society*, 268-269.

Son[83] *iry-pˁt ḥ3ty-ˁ ḫtmty bity smr wˁty rḫ-nswt mˁ3 ḫnmw-ḥtp* (II)

Father[84] *ḥry-tp ˁ3 ḫnmw-ḥtp* (I)

Mother *iryt-pˁt s3t-ipy*

I/4 *bim* [-]

Cairo, JdE 49566 (Baines, *JEA* 72, 1986, 41-53).

Son *iry-pˁt ḥ3ty-ˁ mr pr wr mḥb*

I/5 *mnṯw-ḥr-ḫnt* [-]

Krakow MNK XI-490 (Luft, *ZÄS* 115, 1988).

Husband *3ṯw n ṯt ḥḳ3 nb-iry-r-3w*

Son *3ṯw n ṯt ḥḳ3 sbk-nḫt*

Daughter *ẖkrt-nswt sbk-m-ḥb*

I/6 *nit-iḳrt* [181/27]

Chicago, OIM 8663 (Černy, *IS*, no 98, p. 104-105).

* *wrt ḥts wrt ḥst ḥmt-nṯr ḥtḥr nbt mfk3t*

I/7 *nfrw* [203/17]

Elkab, Tomb 10 (Tylor, *Tomb of Sebeknekht*, pl. 7-10).

Husband *ḥ3ty-ˁ ḫtmty bity mr ḥmw-nṯr sbk-nḫt* (I)[85]

Sons (?) *iry-pˁt ḥ3ty-ˁ mr ḥmw-nṯrw sbk-nḫt* (II)

3ṯw n ṯt ḥḳ3 ḥr-ḥtp

3ṯw n ṯt ḥḳ3 ḥr-m33

3ṯw n ṯt ḥḳ3 sbk-m-s3.f

3ṯw n ṯt ḥḳ3 sbk-nḫt

3ṯw n ṯt ḥḳ3 sbk-nḫt

3ṯw n ṯt ḥḳ3 ///

3ṯw n ṯt ḥḳ3 ///

3ṯw n ṯt ḥḳ3 iy

3ṯw n ṯt ḥḳ3 ptḥ-ḥtp

---

[83] For the list of titles of *ḫnmw-ḥtp* (I), see: Newberry, *Beni Hasan* I, 41-42.

[84] See Newberry, *Beni Hasan* I, 82 (tomb 14).

[85] Cf. Franke, *Doss.*, 565.

ꜣṯw n tt ḥḳꜣ nfr-ḥtp
ꜣṯw n tt ḥḳꜣ nswt
ꜣṯw n tt ḥḳꜣ rn-snb
ꜣṯw n tt ḥḳꜣ tꜣ-mr
ꜣṯw n tt ḥḳꜣ ꜣtḥꜥ

I/8 *nfrw* [203/18][86]
Cairo, GC 20537 (Lange-Schäfer, *CGC* II, 144-145).

Son	*ḥꜣty-ꜥ mr ḥmw-nṯr ḥr-ḥr-ẖwit.f*[87]
Husband	*ḥꜣty-ꜥ ḥr.i*
Daughter-in-law	*iryt-pꜥt sꜣt-nswt sbk-nḫt*

I/9 *nfrw-ꜥnḳt* [203/22]
Jerusalem, Israel Museum 76.31.4498 (Ben-Tor, *The Israel Museum Journal* 7, 1988, 38, no7).[88]

I/10 *nsn* [-][89]
London, BM EA 1348 (*HT* IV, 27).

Son	*sꜣb r nḫn nb-swmnw*

I/11 *rn-snb* [222/26]
Cairo, JdE 75040 (Martin, *Seals*, 828).

I/12 *rdit.n.s* [228/18]
Elkab, Tomb 10 (Tylor, *Tomb of Sebeknekht*, pl. 7-10).

Husband	*iry-pꜥt ḥꜣty-ꜥ mr ḥmw-nṯrw sbk-nḫt*

I/13 *rdit.n.s-n.i* [228/19]
(Kaiser, *MDAIK* 28, 1972, 187-191; Verbovsek, *Private Tempelstatuen,* 345-346).

Husband	*ꜣṯw n tt ḥḳꜣ ii-mr*
Son	*ḫtmty-bity mr gs-pr iy mꜣꜥ-ḫrw*

---

[86] See: Ward, *Feminine Titles*, 54/2.
[87] Cf. Franke, *Doss*., 433.
[88] Another *nfrw-ꜥnḳt* is attested, without any titles, on stela Belin 7288 (*AIB* I, 201).
[89] See: Ward, *Feminine Titles*, 54/16.

I/14 *ḥ3t-špswt* [232/23]

Paris, Louvre C 58 (Awad, *GM* 197, 2003, 43-48; Andreu, *BSAK* 4, 1991, 23).

Husband	*ḫtmty-bity mr 3ḥwt, ddtw*[90]
Sons	*imy-ḫt s3-prw ḥ3-ʿnḫ.f*
	imy-ḫt s3-prw bw-rḫ.f
	ḥri ḫ3wt n imn ib(i)-iʿ(w)
	smsw h3yt ii-ib
	3ṯw n ṯt ḥḳ3 nfr-ḥtp

I/15 *ḥtp-ḥtḥr* [258/23]

El Bersheh, Tomb 1 (Griffith-Newberry, *El Bersheh* II, pl. 23).

**nbt-pr*

Husband:	*iry-pʿt ḥ3ty-ʿ ḥry-tp ʿ3 n wnt ḏhwti-nḫt*[91]

I/16 *ḫty* [277/26]

Beni Hasan, Tomb 23 (Newberry, *Beni Hasan* II, pl. 24).

* *ḥ3tyt-ʿ s3t-ḥ3ty-ʿ nbt-pr rḫt-nswt ḥmt-nṯr ḥtḥr m ʿryt m swt ḥmt-nṯr p3ḫt*

Husband	*ḥ3ty-ʿ mr smywt i3btywt mr ḥmw-nṯr ḫnmw-ḥtp* (II)[92]
Mother	*ṯnt*
Father	*ḥḳ3 n inpwt*
Sons	*iry-pʿt ḥ3ty-ʿ nḫt*[93]

---

[90] Cf. Franke, *Doss.*, 769.

[91] For the complete list of titles see Griffith-Newberry, *El Bersheh* II, 17-25.

[92] The second wife of Khnumhotep (II) was *nbt-pr ṯ3t* who also was 'sealer' and 'keeper of the property of her lord'. She gave birth to three children: *nḥry, ḫnmw-ḥtp* (IV) and to the daughter *s3t-ip*. Cf. Neberry, *Beni Hasan* I, 43-44; Simpson, *JEA* 60, 1974, 102-103; Millard, *Position of Women in the Family and in Society*, 295-296; Ward, in: *Women's Earliest Records*, 36-37; Ward, *GM* 71, 1984, 51-59. Her son Khnumhotep (IV) was the owner of unfinished Beni Hasan tomb no 4 where he is stated as *iry-pʿt ḥ3ty-ʿ ḫnmw-ḥtp ir.n nbt-pr ṯ3t* (Newberry, *Beni Hasan* II, §7), and probably the hair of Khnumhotep (II) as administrator of the Oryx nome (Franke, in: *Middle Kingdom Studies*, 58).

smr wˁty ẖnmw-ḥtp (III)[94]
nḫry
nṯr-nḫt
Daughters ḥmt-nṯr ḥtḥr nbt ˁryt b3kt
ḥmt-nṯr ḥtḥr nbt ˁryt mrt
ḥmt-nṯr p3ḫt nbt st ṯnt

I/17 *s3t-ipy* [285/20]
Beni Hasan, Tomb 14 (Newberry, *Beni Hasan I*, pl. 46).
* *ḥmt ḥḳ3 ḫnt ḥmt nbt nbt-pr*
Husband[95] *iry-pˁt ḥ3ty-ˁ rḫ nswt m3ˁ ḥry-tp 3ˁ n m3-ḥḏ mr ḥnw-nṯr ḫnmw-ḥtp* (I)
Sons *nḫt*
Daughter *iryt-pˁt b3kt*

I/18 *sbk-m-s3.f* [304/7][96]
Paris, Louvre C 6 (Wiedemann, *PSBA* 9, 1887, 191).
Husband *s3-nswt ḫtmty-bity mr gs-pr nbw-ḫˁi.s / ḫnms*[97]
Son *ḫtmty-bity mnṯw-ḥtp*

I/19 *sbk-nḫt* [304/15]
Brooklyn NY, Brooklyn Museum of Fine Arts 43.137 (James, *Corpus of Hieroglyphic Inscriptions* I, pl. 6, 33, no. 87; Romano, *MDAIK* 48, 1992, 131-143).

I/20 *sbk-nḫt* [304/15]
Cairo, JdE 75039 (Martin, *Seals*, 1409).
**nfr ˁnḫ ḏd nfr*

I/21 *sbk-ḥtp* [305/6]

---

[93] *Nḫt* was appointed ruler (*ḥḳ3*) in the Oryx nome by Senwosret II (*Urk.* VII, 31/6).
[94] For his career see Franke, in: *Middle Kingdom Studies*, 51-68.
[95] For the list of titles of *ḥnmw-ḥtp* see: Newberry, *Beni Hasan* I, 82-83.
[96] See Ward, *Feminine Titles*, 54/14; cf. Franke, *Doss.,* 268.
[97] Cf. Schmitz, *Königssohn*, 243, no 12.

London, BM EA 10553 (Winlock, *JEA* 10, 1924, 217-277).

Husband	*mr niwt ṯ3ty mr ḥwt wrt sis snb-ḥnʿ.f*[98]
Daughter	*ḥmt-nswt wrt mnṯw-ḥtp*

I/22 *kwms* [-]

1) Paris, Louvre C 287 [E.13057] (Franke, *JEA* 71, 1985, 175-176 pl. xix).

2) London, BM EA 833 (Clère, *JEA* 68, 1982, 60-68).

**ẖkrt-nswt*

Husband	*sš ḥtpw-nṯr wp-w3wt-iry*
Son	*ḥ3ty-ʿ mr ḥwt-nṯr s3-nswt ṯsw iwʿy n 3bḏw kwms*

I/23 ////

(Martin, *Seals*, 1799).

---

[98] Cf. Franke, *Doss*., 660; 661.

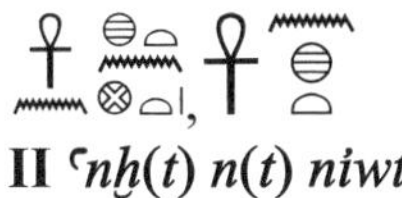

II ʿnḫ(t) n(t) niwt

The term *ʿnḫ n niwt* belongs to the corpus of the regular military titles of the Middle Kingdom and the Second Intermediate Period.[99] During the New Kingdom and later, merely its feminine form occurs as a women's title.[100] In the literature, *ʿnḫ n niwt* is usually rendered as a term that defines a "soldier" of the city regiment,[101] a view that is based on the conclusions of O. D. Berlev. Berlev advocates that the title does not refer to the inhabitants of the towns (*niwt*!) but rather reveals a unique military organisation of the Middle Kingdom – armed forces in which units of young people (*ʿnḫw*) were organised in the frame of a specific territory. [102] These *ʿnḫw nw niwt* could also have been engaged, when needed, in non-military tasks.[103] Berlev pointed out that holders of the title in question belonged to a lower stratum of society.[104]

However, the attestations of the title *ʿnḫ(t) nt niwt* require further study. During the New Kingdom term *ʿnḫt nt niwt*, generally translated as *citizenness* or *townswoman*, has been attested as designation of the free women.[105] It appears in administrative documents, especially in Deir el Medina, as a standard means for designating women. There title might mean as much as 'married

---

[99] Berlev, *RdÉ* 23, 1971, 23-48; Ward, *Titles MK,* 614; Quirke, *RdÉ* 37, 1986, 113; Id., *Administration of Egypt,* 78-79ff; Id., *Titles and bureaux*, 112-113; Stefanović, *Military Organisation*, Ch. V.

[100] Černý, *JEA* 31, 1945, 44; Katary, in: *Agriculture in Egypt*, 61-82; Janssen, in: *Studies Wente*, 185-192.

[101] Berlev, *RdE* 23, 1971, 23-48. Rendered by H. G. Fischer as *townsman, citizen* (*JNES* 16, 1957, 225, n.16; cf. Meeks, *Alex*. I, 66; Ward, *Index MK*, 604) and *stalwart of the town* (Fischer, *Egyptian Studies III*, 131, n.o).

[102] Berlev, *RdÉ* 23, 1971, 40-45; Берлев, *ПС* 17, 1967, 10-11.

[103] Stefanović, *Military Organisation*, Ch. V.

[104] Berlev, *RdÉ* 23, 1971, 40-45; Берлев, *ПС* 17, 1967, 10-11.

[105] Černý, *JEA* 31, 1945, 44; Millard, *Position of Women in the Family and in Society*, 305; Katary, in: *Agriculture in Egypt*, 61-82; Janssen, in: *Studies Wente*, 185-192.

woman'. A. O'Brien suggests that the term perhaps refers to age: *the designation ꜥnḫt nt niwt may have been applied to individuals after certain age.*[106] However, its basic significance is still unclear.[107]

When analysing Middle Kingdom examples, O. D. Berlev presented arguments that the first element of the title (i.e. *ꜥnḫ*) is crucial for its understanding. According to Berlev the *ꜥnḫ / ꜥnḫt* was the designation of a 'young man', or 'young women', and eventually *ꜥnḫt* can be rendered as concubine.[108]

One of Berlev's main arguments, namely that *ꜥnḫt* should be translated as 'concubine', is the case of the lady *rn.s-snb*, attested on the stelae Cairo, CG 20520, Florence 2561 and Florence 2559.[109] The main person on the aforementioned stelae was *wr mḏw šmꜥ imn-m-ḥꜣt*. His father *ḫꜥi-ḫpr-rꜥ-snb* held the title *mr sḫtiw*, while mother, *rn.s-snb* is simply termed *ꜥnḫt*. The fact that she has been labelled neither as *ḥmt* of *wr mḏw šmꜥ imn-m-ḥꜣt,* nor as *nbt-pr* ('married woman'), speaks in Berlev's view in favour of *rn.s-snb* being a concubine (*ꜥnḫt*).[110]

Furthermore, he pointed out that the term *ꜥnḫt* was by mistake treated as an abbreviation of *ꜥnḫt nt niwt* (i.e. the circle, final element of the title, can represent either *ḫ* or *niwt*, and in association with *ꜥnḫ n niwt*, the *niwt* sign was used instead of *ḫ*). Since no certain example of *ꜥnḫt nt niwt* is known from the Middle Kingdom, the 'abbreviated examples' of the title must be, according to him, something else, i.e. *ꜥnḫt.*[111]

However, it seems that even Berlev himself was not completely convinced of the explanation of the position of the lady *rn.s-snb*. In the article entitled *Египетский военный флот в эпоху Среднего*

---

[106] O'Brien, *Women in Demotic Business and Administrative Texts*, 87.

[107] Robins, *Women in Ancient Egypt,* 115; Eyre, *JEA* 93, 2007, 225; Hagen, *ZÄS* 135, 2008, 30-39.

[108] Berlev, *RdE*, 23, 1971, 42; Берлев, *Трудовое население*, 52-53; cf. Millard, *Position of Women in the Family and in Society*, 296-297.

[109] Bostico, *Le Stele Egiz*., no 35, 36 (ANOC 32). *Cf.* Franke, *Doss*., no 336.

[110] Берлев, in: *Проблемы социальных отношений*, 39-40.

[111] Berlev, *RdÉ*, 23, 1972, 42, 23ff*;* Id., *Трудовое население*, 52-53; Id., in: *Проблемы социальных отношений*, 39-41; cf. Millard, *Position of Women in the Family and in Society*, 297, and Ward, *Feminine Titles*, 61.

царства, he noted: “Приводимые там примеры (CM 20520; Firenze 2559, 2561) имеют в виду одно лицо (оно же и на неопубликованной стеле из Рио-де Жанейро), некую *rn.s-snb* или *ꜥnḫt-rn.s-snb*. Если *ꜥnḫt* (так следует читать всю группу знаков перед именем *rn.s-snb*) не часть составного имени, а титул, то это может быть только сокращенный вариант *ꜥnḫt tpt nt nswt*”.[112] Thus, he proposes two explanations: *ꜥnḫt* is either part of the lady’s name or an abbreviated form of her title *ꜥnḫt nt nswt tpt*.

The second link in his argumentation is the woman attested on the stela-chapel Paris, Louvre E 25485. The *ꜥnḫt* (*nt niwt*) *sꜣt-ḥtḥr* was the mother of *mr mšꜥ imny-snb*(*w*) / *imny*. According to Berlev, *sꜣt-ḥtḥr* was of Libyan origin and *ḥmt nswt*. It would be impossible for her to be a legitimate wife of *mr mšꜥ sbk-ḥtp* – she must have been his concubine.[113]

A. Millard notes, among other examples, the *ꜥnḫt* from the tomb of *ḏḥwty-ḥtp* (El Bersheh tomb no 1). *She walks behind one of his daughters and in front of two more. Beside being an ꜥnḫt she is also said to be ‘his beloved who wins his praises every day’, which would be appropriate epithets for a concubine.*[114]

Furthermore, Millard argues that the *ꜥnḫ*(*t*) *n*(*t*) *niwt*, as well as *ꜥnḫt nt nswt tpt*, *were people who for services rendered by them or their families to the state, were entitled to draw at least part of their maintenance, either directly from the royal household or indirectly via the officials of the district in which they lived.*[115]

W. Ward expresses the opinion that Berlev’s initial thesis was incorrect: *five so-called abbreviations cannot be shortened spellings of the anx.t nt niw.t since no example of that title exists in the Middle Kingdom texts. If the title did not exist, it could not be abbreviated; hence the five examples must be read simply as anx.t.*[116] On the other hand, Ward pointed out that there are several clear Middle Kingdom attestations of the title *ꜥnḫt nt niwt* (London, BM EA 833[+ Paris,

[112] Берлев, *ПС* 17, 1967, n. 29.
[113] Берлев, in: *Проблемы социальных отношений*, 35-51.
[114] Millard, *Position of Women in the Family and in Society*, 296-297.
[115] Millard, *Position of Women in the Family and in Society*, 307.
[116] Ward, *Berytus* 31, 1983, 72; Id., *Index MK*, 615, 613.

Louvre E 6167]; London, BM 29447; Cairo, CG 23018 and Cairo, CG 20418).

For Ward, the main problem in the proper understanding of the title is a round sign which could stand either for *ḫ* or *niwt*.[117] In this case, the title can be read in either way. He listed five examples where the round sign appears: Meir, Tomb C 1; El Bersheh, Tomb 1; Florence 2559; Florence 2561; Cairo, CG 20520.[118]

For W. Ward, the case of *rn.s-snb* is not exceptional. On many other Middle Kingdom stelae women who were married and mothers are not called *ḥmt* or *nbt-pr* even *in those cases where both mother and father are figuratively portrayed and specifically identified as the parents*.[119] The evidence that stands directly against rendering *ʿnḫt* as concubine is the existence of the title *ʿnḫt nt nswt tpt*. Ward has recorded six examples of the title in question. As three of the *ʿnḫwt nwt nswt tpwt* were married (London, BM EA 1348; Florence 2554; Athens, National Archaeological Museum, 135), *we can hardly translate ʿnḫt as 'concubine'. It should rather be taken more or less in the literal sense, a "living (female) person"*.[120]

The *ʿnḫt*-person is attested on several examples of the title *ʿnḫt nt niwt* from the Middle Kingdom: London, BM EA 833 (+ Paris, Louvre E 6167) (four women with the title *ʿnḫt nt niwt*; two of them are identified as '*ḥmt.f*'); London, BM 29447; Cairo, CG 23018 (*ʿnḫt nt niwt* as a personal name); Cairo, CG 20418 (written as *ʿnḫ n niwt*).[121] Since the title is written with both *ḫ* and the *niwt* sign in two cases (London, BM EA 29447; Kamal, *ASAE* 4, 1903, 224) Ward noted that this raises *again the problem of whether or not the simple ʿnḫt is really an abbreviated form ʿnḫt nt niwt.* Summing up, Ward accepts Berlev's rendering as simple *ʿnḫt*, but not his translation as 'concubine', since there is no evidence that *ʿnḫt* meant concubine.[122]

---

[117] Ward, *Feminine Titles*, 61.

[118] Ward, *Feminine Titles*, 62.

[119] Ward, *Feminine Titles*, 61, n. 24; *cf.* Ward, *Berytus* 31, 1983, 72-73.

[120] Ward, *Feminine Titles*, 64; cf. Millard, *Position of Women in the Family and in Society*, 305-306.

[121] Ward, *Feminine Titles*, 64.

[122] Ward, *Feminine Titles*, 65.

D. Franke noted that Ward has been probably right in respect of the translation of the *ʿnḫt.*[123] He argued that the title *ʿnḫt* is attested in two cases in the tomb of a nomarch, on the three stelae of ANOC 32, on Cairo, CG 1418, and perhaps on Paris, Louvre E 25485. When analysing the stela London BM EA 833 (+ Paris, Louvre E 6167), Franke concluded that it is the first time that several women attested on the monument in question are called *ʿnḫt nt niwt*; these examples *must have the meaning of 'townswomen' as later in the New Kingdom.*[124]

The attestations of the title recorded on the aforementioned stela are of special importance because two of the *ʿnḫt nt niwt*[125] are labelled as *ḥmt.f* – their husband was *imy-ḫnt sʿnḫ-ptḥ*. Another woman with the same title is called his sister.[126] The title of *sʿnḫ-ptḥ* (*chamberlain – he who is in the Outer Palace*)[127] perhaps points to the high palace official; on a stela he is depicted behind king Rahotep, while the king presents offerings to Osiris. However, female members of his family were not so prominent. Not that his wives were *ʿnḫt nt niwt*, the mother of *sʿnḫ-ptḥ* is termed as *nmḥyt.*

The *nmḥyt* is another designation of free women, which may belong to a group or collective[128]. Beside the single designation *nmḥyt* (*w3dt-hw* [BM EA 833]), there are several extensions to the title: *nmḥyt nt niwt*, '*nmḥyt* of the town',[129] (*rn.s-snb* [Cairo, CG 20104; commissioned by *rḫ nswt rḥw-ʿnḫ*], *nbt* [Cairo, CG 20266; commissioned by *sš n ḫnt kki*], name lost [Cairo, CG 20392; commissioned by *mr ḥtp-nṯr sbk-ḥtp*], *bbi* [Tübingen 459,

[123] Franke, *JEA* 76, 1990, 230.

[124] Franke, *JEA* 71, 1985, 175-176; cf. Берлев, in: *Проблемы социальных отношений*, 41.

[125] Cf. II/1, and II/3.

[126] Cf. II/9.

[127] Ward, *Index MK*, 425; Fischer, *Egyptian Titles of the Middle Kingdom*, 50; Quirke, *Titles and Bureaux*, 34.

[128] Ward, *Feminine Titles*, 6-7; Millard, *Position of Women in the Family and in Society*, 308-309; Franke, *JEA* 76, 1990, 228-229; Kóthay, *Acta Antiqua Academiae Scientiarum Hungaricae* 46, 2006, 155-164 (cf. p. 157 with the list of attestations).

[129] Ward, *Index MK,* 830.

commissioned by *mr st n šnꜥ ꜥꜣ imny*], *mm* and *tt*[130] [Padua, Museo Civico di Padova])[131]; *nmḥyt n ḥry-pr*, '*nmḥyt* of the domestic-servant,[132] (*ḥpyw*, *bbi-šrit* and *bbi-wꜣḏt* [Brooklyn 08.480.176, commissioned by several people], *nmḥyt nt ẖrtyw-nṯr wꜥrt mḥtt,* '*nmḥyt* of the necropolis-workers of the northern district',[133] (*wpwt*-list of P. London, UC 32163), *nmḥyt nt ẖrtyw-nṯr,* '*nmḥyt* of the necropolis-workers' (*tt* [Swiss, Private collection, commissioned for *wr mḏw šmꜥ ṯni-ꜥnḫ*])[134] and *nmḥyt n*(*t*) n'*t* (*nbt-iwnt* and *nn.i-rs* [Cortona 348]).[135]

Among the attested *nmḥywt*, three are of special importance. The *nmḥyt nt niwt*, recorded on stela CG 20392, bears the title *nbt-pr*. A 'freewomen of the town' mentioned on CG 20266 is a member of an extensive family. She is termed as beloved sister of *sš n ḫnt kki ms.n nbt-pr iy*. Beside *kki*, there are two more brothers and one sister (*nbt-pr sbk-ḥr-ḥb*). Their (?) father *rs.f* held the title *mr pr*. He is probably also attested on stela Cairo, CG 20581 among the members of the family of his father.

The main person on the stela Tübingen 459 is *mr st n šnꜥ ꜥꜣ imny*. His wife *bbi* bears the title *nmḥyt nt niwt*(compare plate 1).It has been already recognised that some members of *imny*'s family, including himself, are attested on stela Oxford, QC 1111.[136] Beside the names and titles of *imny*'s father (?) (*mr st n šnꜥ ꜥꜣ imbw*) and brother (*mr st n ꜥbꜣ iḫt imbw*) there are two ladies: *nbt-pr sḥnt* and *nbt-pr bbi*. The *nbt-pr sḥnt*, recorded on Tübingen 459 without any titles, is the mother of *nmḥyt nt niwt bbi*. She was perhaps the wife of *mr wꜥrt n gnwtyw ptḥ-pw-wꜣḥ.*[137] The second lady on QC 1111, *nbt-pr bbi*, is more puzzling, as there are three women with the same

---

130 Uncertain reading.

131 Dolzani, in: *Viaggatori veneti alla scoperta dell'Egitto*, 175[1], fig.

132 Ward, *Index MK,* 831.

133 Ward, *Index MK,* 832.

134 Page-Gasser, *Ägypten*, 100-102.

135 Botti, *Museo dell' Accademia di Cortona*, 86-87, pl. IX. Cf. Franke, *JEA* 76, 1990, 228.

136 See: Franke, *Doss.,* 71, 95, 420.

137 He is perhaps also attested (with the title *mr wꜥrt n gnwtyw*) on London, UC 34347.

name on Tübingen 459: the mother (*nbt-pr bbỉ*), wife (*nmḥyt nt nỉwt bbỉ*) and daughter (*nbt-pr bbỉ*) of *ỉmny*. By *bbỉ*'s position on the stela QC 1111, I am more inclined to recognise her as the wife of *mr st n šnꜥ ꜥꜣ ỉmny*. If this is true, *bbỉ* would be the second *nmḥyt nt nỉwt* holding the title *nbt-pr*.

The masculine *nmḥ* is usually rendered, depending on context and epoch, as a term which defines a social class ('freeman'), a person of a low socio-economic standing ('poor man'), and orphan. The feminine *nmḥyt*, most often attested as an element of titles (*nmḥyt* + X), is usually translated as 'ward' (i.e. the term denoted women without natural male protector),[138] 'freewomen' (especially in respect to the New Kingdom documents),[139] and widow.[140]

K. A. Kóthay points out that the term was applied to the small group of women attached to a settlement or a group of men with the same occupation; *it can not be considered as a designation referring to a well defined category of the population having any privileges or special legal capacities*.[141] Kóthay recognises, as well as Ward before her, that, in some instances, *nmḥyt* has been not without male 'protector' (husband / brother / grandson), and that they belonged to the households of the male relatives.[142] According to Kóthay, a term *nmḥyt* indicates their social status within the household – they were widowed or orphaned female relatives.[143] In cases of CG 20392 and Tübingen 459 Kóthay suggests that the title *nmḥyt nt nỉwt* should be considered as an designation of secondary importance as *the other titles* (*ḥmt.f* and *nbt-pr*) *born by the women appear to indicate their actual status, that is, they were housewives* – they were widows who

---

[138] Griffith, *Kahun Papyri*, 21, n. 34; Collier-Quirke, *The UCL Lahun Papyri: Religious*, 111.

[139] Ward, *Feminine Titles*, 9. Cf. Katary, *Land Tenure*, 211 (with further references).

[140] Kóthay, *Acta Antiqua Academiae Scientiarum Hungaricae* 46, 2006, 155-164.

[141] Kóthay, *Acta Antiqua Academiae Scientiarum Hungaricae* 46, 2006, 159.

[142] Kóthay, *Acta Antiqua Academiae Scientiarum Hungaricae* 46, 2006, 159; cf. Ward, *Feminine Titles*, 9.

[143] Kóthay, *Acta Antiqua Academiae Scientiarum Hungaricae* 46, 2006, 159.

remarried following the death of their former spouses keeping their status as *nmḥyt*.[144] Being *nmḥyt*, and as such very vulnerable, a woman would have had some benefits associated with the community she was attached to: the town or groups of people. They appear to be beneficiaries of revenues, as in case of the *nmḥywt* attested in the household listing from Lahun (UC 32163), which may have originated in the local community, *i.e. in contracts between a private contractor and the city, or from the contracts between private persons.*[145]

The term *nmḥyt n ḥry-pr* has been discussed by Berlev. He proposes, pointing to the stela Brooklyn 08.480.176, that the domestic servants of the palace were responsible for daughters of their late colleagues.[146]

Whether widows[147] or wards, two *nmḥyt nt* n'*t* recorded on stela Cortona 348 and *nmḥyt nt ẖrtyw-nṯr* on stela published by M. Page-Gasser are of special importance. The stela Cortona 348 has a lunette (A) and two registers (B, C). Under the lunette is a text consisting of an offering formula on behalf of *nmḥyt nt* n'*t nn.ỉ-rs*, the main person of the stela. Register A displays two figures facing one another, separated by the captions. The right half is covered by the figure of a sitting *nn.ỉ-rs* facing left. The kneeling figure shown to the left is *sn.s wp-w3wt* (?). Register B displays two kneeling figures facing one another, separated by the captions: *nmḥyt nt* n'*t nbt-ỉwnt* and *nbt-pr ḥr-bỉ* (?). It is difficult to make out the exact relationship of the other two women to *nn.ỉ-rs*.

Stela Cortona 348 belongs to a woman. Although feminine stelae[148] may not spell out the women's role in the family and society

---

[144] Kóthay, *Acta Antiqua Academiae Scientiarum Hungaricae* 46, 2006, 159.

[145] Kóthay, *Acta Antiqua Academiae Scientiarum Hungaricae* 46, 2006, 161-164.

[146] Берлев, *Общественные отношения,* 153-155.

[147] It is important to note that *ẖ3rt* (*Wb* III 363.4-7) is the regular term for 'widow' (i.e. a window without support, in need of protection) in Egyptian wisdom literature. .

[148] The number of attestations is probably not definite; see Stefanović, *GM* 218, 2008, 81-92 and Id. *GM* 220, 2009, 95-98.

of the Middle Kingdom, they show that about 80% of female owners or main persons are identified by title. Many of these women were called *nbt-pr*, while others belong to the *ẖkrt-nswt* (Bristol H 521; Franke, *Heqaib*, 87, Tf. 9; Lutz, *Egyptian Tomb Steles*, no 80), *wbꜣyt* (London, UC 14360), and *ḥst* (Cairo, CG 20257). It is also interesting to note that almost 90% of the stelae belonging to a woman did not give her male family members name, including husbands.

The *nmḥyt nt ẖrtyw-nṯr tt* is recorded as a mother of *wr mḏw šmꜥ ṯni-ꜥnẖ* on the stela which was commissioned by his brother *imy-ẖt rn.f-rs*.[149] Thus, she was not without 'natural male protector', and her husband was perhaps also alive. The same is true for *nmḥyt nt niwt mm*, the wife of 'overseer of the department of the chamber of bread' (*mr st n ꜥt t*) *rḥw-snb*, recorded on a stela from the Museo Civico di Padova.

If Kóthay is right in her hypothesis that being *nmḥyt* implies specific situations of acquiring property and incomes, it would be expectable to find them widely attested in various administrative documents. The highly limited number of attestations, almost all of them being on stelae, do not support any conclusion about their social standing. From the late Old Kingdom on it had been typical for certain professions to stay in the family. A woman who inherited a 'job' could pass it to her son, or / and acquire certain benefits or only receive income as, for example, '*nmḥyt* of the necropolis workers'. Whatever the answers to these and many related questions, the Middle Kingdom *nmḥyt* could be married, could commission (?) a stela for herself, could have family members (both male and female) that wear a title; the social implications of their titles (*nmḥyt* + X) certainly should be considered, but contemporary sources do not provide us with clear answers.

The late Middle Kingdom lady *ini*[150] is also worth of notice. She belonged to the family of *ḥry-pr iy* (who seems to be of great

[149] Page-Gasser, *Ägypten*, 100-102.

[150] Habachi, *Elephantine* IV, no 81, 100, pl. 197; Franke, *Heqaib,* 85; cf. II/2.

importance to the owner on the monument *s3b nb-iw*) and held the title *ʿnḫt nt niwt* at the end of the XIII Dynasty: [151]

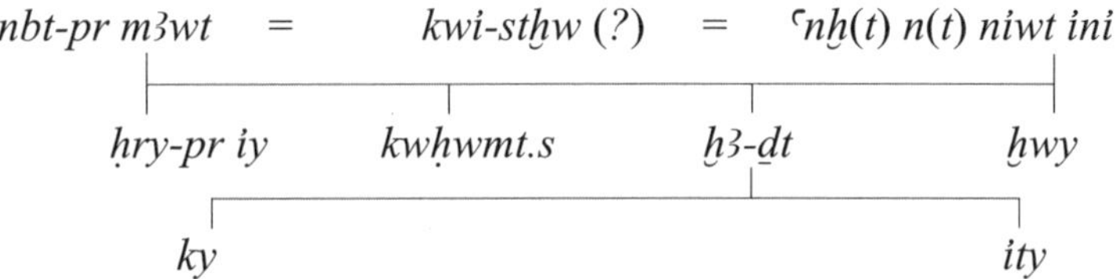

The lady *t3-nw* [*t3t*], recorded on the statuette Linköping Museum 156[152] held two titles: *nbt-pr* and *ʿnḫ*(*t nt niwt*). Her son *ẖty* was an *ʿnḫ n niwt*.[153] The first title of *t3-nw* [*t3t*] is clearly readable, but the second is either *ʿnḫ*(*t*) or *ʿnḫ*(*t nt niwt*). The case of the lady *t3-nw* [*t3t*] is worth of being noted as there is a second title attached to a woman labelled as *ʿnḫt* (*nt niwt*), implying, in this case, that she was a 'mistress of the house'.

As for the meaning of her first title, I'm inclined to treat all *ʿnḫt* titles as an abbreviation of *ʿnḫt nt niwt*. In writing of the male counterpart of the title (i.e. *ʿnḫ n niwt*), the final element is in most cases the 'circle' sign, but we treat it regularly as the *niwt* sign. If there was 'one rule' for the orthography of the male title, why would 'another rule' be used for the spelling of its feminine version. It is important to note that the female counterpart of the male title can not be treated and understood as a mere 'transposition' – the realms of men and women were in most cases completely different and the 'same' titles may imply different duties and responsibilities (as in the case of *wb3* / *wb3yt*; *ʿḳ* / *ʿḳyt*, etc.). Furthermore, J.J. Jansen wrote in respect of examples from Deir el-Medina of the title *ʿnḫt nt niwt*: "The spelling varies, a conspicuous and rather frequent variant being plural strokes after *niwt* as if the inhabitants of the City were designated. A common abbreviation is *ʿnḫ-niwt*, or even simply *ʿnḫ*."[154] The same can be true for the Late Middle Kingdom and Second Intermediate Period examples.

---

[151] See Franke, *Heqaib*, 85.

[152] Björkman, *Linköping Museum*, 25-26; cf. II/12.

[153] Stefanović, *Military Titles*, 167.

[154] Janssen, in: *Studies Wente*, 186.

The Late Middle Kingdom title *ꜥnḫt nt niwt* is not revealing in terms of social status, and it is hard to conclude anything about its precise meaning and social implications. The titles of the husbands of these women include *imy-ḫnt*, *ḥry-pr*, *mr sḫtiw*, and perhaps *mr mšꜥ* and *wr mḏw šmꜥ*.[155] A. Gardiner in his *Ramesside Administrative Documents* simply renders the title as 'lady',[156] and this is, I think, the most adequate translation.

II/1 *iꜥ-ib* [11/19]
London, BM EA 833 (+ Paris, Louvre E 6167) (*HT* IV, pl. 24; Clère, *JEA* 68, 1982, 60-68).
Husband *imy-ḫnt sꜥnḫ-ptḥ*

II/2 *ini*[157] [33/4]
(Habachi, *Elephantine* IV, no 81).
Husband (?) *ḥri-pr iii*

II/3 *id* [53/12]
London, BM EA 833 (+ Paris, Louvre E 6167) (*HT* IV, pl. 24; Clère, *JEA* 68, 1982, 60-68).
Husband *imy-ḫnt sꜥnḫ-ptḥ*

II/4 *ꜥꜣ-ḥtp* ? [416/21]
Meir, Tomb C 1 (Blackman, *Meir* VI, 10, pl. 13).

II/5 *ꜥnḫ-ib* [62/23]
Genf 51 (Wiedemann - Pörtner, *AG* III, Taf. II/3).

II/6 *nḏm-tꜣw.s* [215/22]

155 Cf. Millard, *Position of Women in the Family and in Society*, 307.
156 Gardiner, *Wilbour Papyrus* II, 76.
157 Contra Stefanović, *Military Titles*, n. 34

London, BM EA 833 (+ Paris, Louvre E 6167) (*HT* IV, pl. 24; Clère, *JEA* 68, 1982, 60-68).

II/7 *rn.s-snb* [224/1]
1) Florence 2561 (Bostico, *Le Stele Egiz.*, no 36; ANOC 32).[158]
2) Florence 2559 (Bostico, *Le Stele Egiz.*, no 35; ANOC 32).
3) Cairo, GC 20520 (Lange-Schäfer, *CGC* II, 116-122)

Husband ?	*mr sḫtyw ḫʿi-ḫpr-rʿ-snb*
Son	*wr mḏw šmʿ imn-m-ḥ3t / nḥy*

II/8 *s3t-ḥtḥr* [291/14]
Paris, Louvre E 25485 (Vandier, *Revue du Louvre* 13, 1963, 1-10).

Husband	*mr mšʿ sbk-ḥtp*
Son	*mr mšʿ imny-snb(w) / imny*

II/9 *s3(t)-tp-iḥw* [294/16]
London, BM EA 833 (+ Paris, Louvre E 6167) (*HT* IV, pl. 24; Clère, *JEA* 68, 1982, 60-68)

Brother	*imy-ḫnt sʿnḫ-ptḥ*
Mother (?)	*nmḥyt w3ḏt-hw*

II/10 *snb.f-n(.i)* [314/8]
London, BM EA 250 (*HT* IV, 40).

II/11 *ddt.s* [403/18] (?)
Athens, National Archaeological Museum 154 (Pörtner, *Athen und Konstantinopel*, IV/11).

II/12 *t3-nw* [*t3t*] [-]
Linköping Museum, Sweden 156 (St) (Björkman, *Linköping Museum*, 25-26).

**nbt-pr*	
Son	*ʿnḫ n niwt ḫty*

II/13 *ṯi3by* [-]
London, BM EA 29447 (Martin, *Seals*, 1735).

---

[158] Cf. Franke, *Doss.*, no 336.

II/14 ///
El Bersheh, Tomb 1 (Griffith-Newberry, *El Bersheh* I, 37).

III *ꜥnẖt nt nswt tpt*

The holders of the Middle Kingdom title *ꜥnẖt nt nswt tpt*[159] seem to have been of the same rank as the 'King's Ornaments' or the 'Servants of the Ruler' and some of them were perhaps attached to the residence, either at Memphis, Thebes or Itj-tawy.[160] Some of the holders of the title were married women. Information on the titles of their family members suggests the high social status of the *ꜥnẖt nt nswt tpt*. Among the male members of their families, the most prominent place belongs to the holders of the title of *wr mḏw šmꜥ* and of various military titles.

Title	Father	Husband	Son	Brother
ꜣṯw n ṯt ḥḳꜣ				
sꜣb r nẖn				
ꜣṯw ꜥꜣ n nỉwt				
sḥḏ šmsw				
šmsw				
rẖ nswt mꜣꜥ				
wr mḏw šmꜥ				
sš n ẖnrt wr				
smsw hꜣyt				
ỉry-pḏt				

[159] Ward, *Index MK*, 616. Cf. Millard, *Position of Women in the Family and in Society*, 305.
[160] Franke, *JEA* 76, 1990, 231. Cf. Ward, *Feminine Titles*, 62-64 and Berlev, *RdÉ* 23, 1971, 25-26.

The *wr mḏw šmˁ* is one of the most common regular titles of the late Middle Kingdom and Second Intermediate Period.[161] A holder of this title was perhaps an official attached to the vizier's bureau.[162] The high number of holders of the title *wr mḏw šmˁ* may point to their social standing close to the court circles.
The family of the *ˁnḫt nt nswt tpt nfrw* (III/10), recorded on the late Middle Kingdom stela Florence 2553 shows a high concentration of military titles: her husband was an *sš n ḫnrt wr*, one of their (?) sons was archer (*iry-pḏt wsr-nšmt*)[163] while three other brother are labelled as *smsw h3yt*. Some of the holders of the title *smsw h3yt* may also belong to the 'military circle' as they were part of the palace entourage[164](compare plate 2). A similar case is exemplified within the "military family" recorded on the stela Moscow 5608: here the *men under arms* have been attested through three generations.[165]

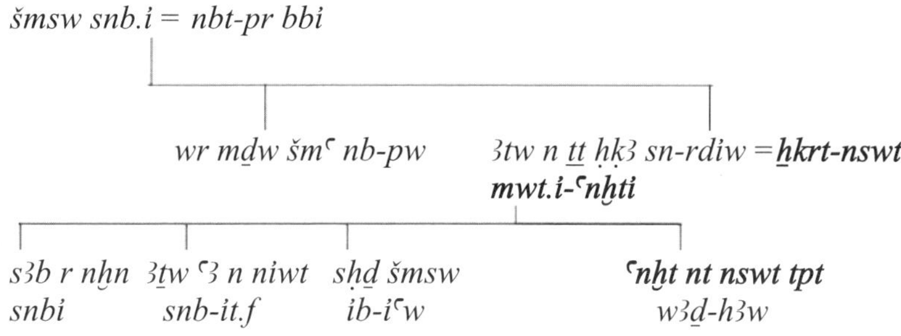

[161] Ward, *Index MK*, no 721; Quirke, *Titles and Bureaux*, 87; Id., in: *RdÉ* 37, 1986, 113, 120.
[162] Grajetzki, *Zentralverwaltung*, 39ff.
[163] One *šmsw ˁryt* is also attested on the monument (Stefanović, *Military Titles*, nos 308, 794, 909; Id. *WZKM* 98, 2008, 243)
[164] Quirke, *Titles and bureaux*, 33.
[165] See Stefanović, *Military Titles*, nos 306, 465, 724, 843; Id. *WZKM*, 98, 2008, 245-246.

However, very little is known about the specifics of the title *ꜥnḫt nt nswt tpt*. The number of women who held the title in question was comparatively small.[166]

III/1 ***ꜥꜣ-///*** [-]
Shalfak 31-3-200 [B 7686] (Dunham - Janssen, *SCF* II, pl. 61B).

III/2 ***wꜣḏ-hꜣw*** [74/24]
Moscow 5608 (Hodjash - Berlev, *Pushkin Museum*, no 38).

Father	*ꜣṯw n ṯt ḥḳꜣ sn-rdiw*
Mother	*ḫkrt-nswt mwt.i-ꜥnḫti*
Brothers	*sꜣb r nḫn snbi*
	ꜣṯw ꜥꜣ n niwt snb-it.f
	sḥḏ šmsw ib-iꜥw

III/3 ***mwt-p(w)-snb***[167] [-]
Bolton 1920.10.12 (ex 10.20.12) (Stefanović, *SAK* 2009).

Father	*šmsw ddi*
Mother ?	*bꜣkt nt ḥḳꜣ mwt-pw-snb*
Brothers	*rḫ nswt mꜣꜥ rn-snb*
	wr mḏw šmꜥ nb-swmnw
	wr mḏw šmꜥ rs-snb
	wr mḏw šmꜥ rn-snb
Sisters	*nbt-pr nfr-ḥtp*
	ꜥnḫt nt nswt tpt nfr-ḥtp

III/4 ***nbw-m-ḥꜣt*** [191/4]
Moscow 5608 (Hodjash - Berlev, *Pushkin Museum*, no 38).

III/5 ***nbw-ḥr-ḫnit*** [191/22]
1) Cairo, CG 20481 (Lange-Schäfer, *CGC* II, 76-77).

---

[166] Compare with Berlev's list of attestation in: Берлев, *ПС* 17, 1967, 11. See also Millard, *Position of Women in the Family and in Society*, 306-307.
[167] Cf. Ward, *Feminine Titles*, 64.

2) Cairo, CG 20743[168] (Lange-Schäfer, *CGC* II, 376-377).

III/6 *nbt-mr* [-]
Athens, National Archaeological Museum, 135 (Pörtner, *Athen und Konstantinopel*, Tf. III/10).

Husband	*wr mḏw šmꜥ sn.i͗-rs*
Son (?)	*wr mḏw šmꜥ dd.tw-sbk*

III/7 *nfr-ḥtp*[169] [198/14]
1) London, UC 11438 (Martin, *Seals*, 715).
2) Bolton 1920.10.12 (ex 10.20.12) (Stefanović, *SAK* 2009).

Father	*šmsw ddi͗*
Mother ?	*bꜣkt nt ḥḳꜣ mwt-pw-snb*
Brothers	*rḫ nswt mꜣꜥ rn-snb*
	wr mḏw šmꜥ nb-swmnw
	wr mḏw šmꜥ rs-snb
	wr mḏw šmꜥ rn- snb
Sisters	*nbt-pr nfr-ḥtp*
	ꜥnḫt nt nswt tpt mwt-p(w)-snb

III/8 *nfrt-i͗w* ? [201/13]
1) Cairo, CG 20481 (Lange-Schäfer, *CGC* II, 76-77).
2) Cairo, CG 20743[170] (Lange-Schäfer, *CGC* II, 376-377).

III/9 *rn-snb* [222/26]
1) Cairo, CG 20481 (Lange-Schäfer, *CGC* II, 76-77).
2) Cairo, CG 20743[171] (Lange-Schäfer, *CGC* II, 376-377).
Husband ?

III/10 *nfrw* [203/2]
Florence 2553 (Bostico, *Le Stele Egiz.*, no 34).

Husband	*sš n ḫnrt wr sꜣ-ptḥ*
Son ?	*i͗ry-pḏt wsr-nšmt*

[168] Maspero, *ZÄS* 20, 1882, 122-123.
[169] Cf. Ward, *Feminine Titles*, 64.
[170] Maspero, *ZÄS* 20, 1882, 122-123.
[171] Maspero, *ZÄS* 20, 1882, 122-123.

smsw h3yt ddw-nšmt
smsw h3yt nfr-nšmt
smsw h3yt 3ḫ-n.i- imn-ḥtp

III/11 ***snb-sn*** [314/18]
London, BM EA 1348 (*HT* IV, 27; Bourriau, *Pharaohs and Mortals*, no 45).

Husband	*3ṯw n ṯt ḥḳ3 s3-ḥtḥr*
Son	*s3b r nḫn ib-iʿw*

III/12 ***stt-m-ḥb*** [-]
Clandeboye Collection 6 (Edwards, *JEA* 51, 1965, 27).

IV *ʿḥʿyt*

In comparison with other regular feminine servant titles, the title *ʿḥʿyt* is seldom attested. All attestations, except Cairo, CG 20476, belong to the early Middle Kingdom. Women with the title *ʿḥʿyt* are found in most cases among offering bearers and servants presenting food, cloth and other offerings. The exception is again stela Cairo, CG 20476 where one *ʿḥʿyt* presents incense to the deceased, *wr mḏw šmʿ iw-ṯni*, though this function is performed elsewhere by other categories of servants.[172]

The women with the title *ʿḥʿyt* are attested on the monuments commissioned by *mr ʿẖnwty* (Paris, Louvre C 196; Cairo, CG 20026), *mr ʿẖnwty n pr mꜣʿt* (Paris, Louvre C 166), *mr pr* (Cairo, CG 20542) and *wr mḏw šmʿ* (Cairo, CG 20476).[173] From their position among other servants and representations on monuments, O.D. Berlev concluded that *ʿḥʿyt* belong to the group of *ḥryt-pr* servants.[174] However, we do not know much about their duties, nor their social background. No members of their families are attested.

IV/1 *ḥpw* [238/14]
Paris, Louvre C196 (Gayet, *Stèles de la XIIe dyn.*, pl. 24).

IV/2 *st-imn* [279/21][175]
Cairo, CG 20542 (Lange-Schäfer, *CGC* II, 163-164; ANOC 4).

IV/3 *sꜣt-ptḥ* [288/22]

---

[172] Ward, *Index MK*, 626; Ward, *Feminine Titles*, 5; Millard, *Position of Women in the Family and in Society*, 322; Gardiner, *Sinuhe*, 110.
[173] Cf. Берлев, *Общественные отношения*, 160-161.
[174] Берлев, *Общественные отношения*, 161; cf. Берлев, *Трудовое население*, 325.
[175] Cf. Берлев, *Общественные отношения*, 161.

Cairo, GC 20476 (Lange-Schäfer, *CGC* II, 73-74).

IV/4 ***s3t-ḥtḥr*** [291/14]
Paris, Louvre C196 (Gayet, *Stèles de la XIIe dyn.*, pl. 24).

IV/5 ***k3yt*** [341/22]
Paris, Louvre C166 (Gayet, *Stèles de la XIIe dyn.*, pl. 26).

IV/6 ***ddt-nbw*** [403/14]
Paris, Louvre C166 (Gayet, *Stèles de la XIIe dyn.*, pl. 26).

IV/7 ***ddt-nbw*** [403/14]
Cairo, GC 20026 (Lange-Schäfer, *CGC* I, 33-34).

IV/8 ***ṯ3-ḥmt*** ? [365/16]
Turin 1626 (1534) Maspero, *RT* 3, 1882, 115-117, no 107).

V ʿḳyt

The title *ʿḳyt*, 'female enterer',[176] belongs to the regular feminine titles of the Middle Kingdom. Women entitled as *ʿḳywt* are attested among household servants and offering bearers only.[177] W. Ward notes that, judging from the male counterpart, these servants were perhaps allowed to enter the private family quarters.[178] Since they are always represented in the context of food preparation and delivery - some of them are shown shaping loaves of bread - it is clear that they were attached to the provisioning sector of the estate, i.e. to the *šnʿ*.[179] It seems that *ʿḳywt* duties were similar to those performed by *wbꜣywt*, *ʿḥʿywt* and *ẖtwt-prw*. As the other classes of servants, *ʿḳywt* were *meryt*-people, i.e. they were *ḥmwt*.[180]

A group of *ʿḳywt* represented in the tomb of Djar (TT 366) as preparing food has been highlighted by C. H. Roehrig and M. Lorenz.[181] The identification of these women by name and title is exceptional for Roehrig, because otherwise *women from the lower classes are generally not identified as individuals. They appear in generic scenes on walls and in funerary models, and sometimes are accompanied by a short text describing their activity – servant,*

---

[176] Ward, *Index MK* 635; Millard, *Position of Women in the Family and in Society*, 321; Берлев, *Общественные отношения*, 259.

[177] Ward, *Feminine Titles*, 6; Millard, *Position of Women in the Family and in Society*, 321; Берлев, *Общественные отношения*, 259-260.

[178] Ward, *Feminine Titles*, 6.

[179] For *šnʿ / pr šnʿ* see Берлев, *Общественные отношения* and Quirke, *Titles and bureaux*, 65; Roehrig, in: *Mistress of the House, Mistress of Heaven: Women in Ancient Egypt*, 14; Szpakowska, *Daily Life in Ancient Egypt*, 91-98; Lorenz, in: *The Life of Meresamun*, 101).

[180] Берлев, *Общественные отношения*, 260.

[181] Roehrig, in: *Mistress of the House, Mistress of Heaven: Women in Ancient Egypt*, 14; Lorenz, in: *The Life of Meresamun*, 101.

baker, weaver, spinner.[182] Furthermore, *these female figures, and their male counterparts, function more as hieroglyphs than as representations of real people.*[183] According to Roehrig, the women from Djar's tomb are known to us because their master decided to name them in his tomb, which was perhaps a *way for a wealthy man to provide for his dependents.* She also noted that artistically these women's figures are merely generic, crude representations.[184]

Lorenz also pointes to the fact that a scene from TT 366 *is unusual in that these women are identified by name, along with the title "servant". Presumably, they were employees of the tomb owner who worked either for his personal estate or for the king's "harem" (or private apartments), where the tomb owner himself was employed.*[185] However, general evidence does not support this opinion.

The thirty-seven holders of the title *ꜥḳyt* are attested on monuments of the Middle Kingdom.[186] The majority of them are recorded on stelae among the servants and offering bearers belonging to the estate of their employer. All of them have been identified by title and name, so the examples from the tomb of Djar are not exceptional and unique even in respect of tombs.[187] Furthermore, on several Middle Kingdom stelae the owner specifically states that he included his relatives, friends and servants. One of the best examples is the family stela Paris, Louvre C 173 with the formulation: *h3w nb*(*w*) *snw nb*(*w*) *ẖnmsw nb*(*w*) *ḏt nbt nt pr m iw*(*t*) *r bw nti im.*[188]

---

[182] Roehrig, in: *Mistress of the House, Mistress of Heaven: Women in Ancient Egypt*, 14.

[183] Roehrig, in: *Mistress of the House, Mistress of Heaven: Women in Ancient Egypt*, 14.

[184] Roehrig, in: *Mistress of the House, Mistress of Heaven: Women in Ancient Egypt*, 14.

[185] Lorenz, in: *The Life of Meresamun*, 101, n. 19 (quoting Roehrig, in: *Mistress of the House, Mistress of Heaven: Women in Ancient Egypt*, 14-15).

[186] Compare with Berlev's and Millard's list of attestations (Берлев, *Общественные отношения*, 260; id. Берлев, *Трудовое население*, 325; Millard, *Position of Women in the Family and in Society*, 321).

[187] See Davies, *Antefoker*, pl. 12.

[188] See Franke, *AVB*, 219-220, 257-262.

None of the ꜥḳywt-servants bear any other titles. The members of their families are very seldom attested and, as a rule, without any titles. From the earliest Middle Kingdom occurrences of the title until the latest, it is clear that the title-holders were of very poor social standing.

V/1 *iwḥt-ib* [18/17]
Cairo, CG 20582 (Lange-Schäfer, *CGC* II, 222).
Mother *mwt.s*

V/2 *ipi* [22/15]
Cairo, CG 20516 (Lange-Schäfer, *CGC* II, 111).

V/3 *ipi* [22/15]
TT 60 (Davies, *Antefoker*, pl. 12).

V/4 *ippi* [24/7]
Cairo, CG 20441 (Lange-Schäfer, *CGC* II, 39).

V/5 *inpw-m-s3.s* [37/13]
Cairo, CG 20400 (Lange-Schäfer, *CGC* II, 1).

V/6 *id* [53/12]
Turin 1626 (1534) (Maspero, *RT* 3, 1882, 115-117, no 107).
Daughter *s3-ẖnmw*

V/7 *ꜥnẖw* [68/6]
Paris, Louvre C170 (E3110) (Gayet, *Stèles de la XIIe dyn.*, pl. 27-28).

V/8 *bb* [95/8]
Paris, Louvre C170 (E3110) (Gayet, *Stèles de la XIIe dyn.*, pl. 27-28).

V/9 *ppi* [131/12]
London, BM EA 129 (*HT* II, 43).

V/10 ***mwt.sn*** [-]
Paris, Louvre C173 (Gayet, *Stèles de la XIIe dyn.*, pl. 29).
Mother *sʿnḫ*

V/11 ***mrt-ỉtf.s*** [158/18]
Cairo, CG 20026 (Lange-Schäfer, *CGC* I, 33-34).
Son *ỉmny*
nḫt-sbk

V/12 ***mkt*** [166/19]
TT 366 (Winlock, *Excavations at Deir el Bahar*, pl. 17/7).

V/13 ***nḫt-ḥmt*** [209/18]
Paris, Louvre C15 (Gayet, *Stèles de la XIIe dyn.*, pl. 54).
**ʿḳyt.f nt st ỉb.f*

V/14 ***rn.s-ʿnḫ*** [223/20]
Cairo, CG 20441 (Lange-Schäfer, *CGC* II, 39).

V/15 ***rḥwt-ʿnḫ*** [226/2]
Paris, Louvre C166 (Gayet, *Stèles de la XIIe dyn.*, pl. 26).

V/16 ***ḥpy*** [238/6]
London, BM EA 829 (*HT* IV, 5).
Daughter *nḏm*

V/17 ***ḥpw*** [238/14]
Cairo, CG 20456 (Lange-Schäfer, *CGC* II, 51-54).

V/18 ***ḥnṯw*** [245/15]
Aix-en-Provence, Musée Granet 6 (Tesurus Linguae Aegyptie: DZA 22.024.520).

V/19 ***s3t-ỉmn*** [286/6]
London, BM EA 1322 (*HT* III, 33).

V/20 ***s3t-ỉmn*** [286/6]
Leiden 4 (V 6) (Boeser, *Leiden* II, pl. 8).

V/21 ***s3t-ỉn-ḥrt*** [286/14]
TT 366 (Winlock, *Excavations at Deir el Bahar*, pl. 17/7).

V/22 ***s3t-pp*** ? [288/18]
TT 366 (Winlock, *Excavations at Deir el Bahar*, pl. 17/7).

V/23 ***s3t-ḫnti-ḫty*** [292/21]
Cairo, CG 20516 (Lange-Schäfer, *CGC* II, 111).

V/24 ***s3t-tp-ỉḥw*** [294/16]
TT 60 (Davies, *Antefoker*, pl. 12)

Daughter	*s3t-ỉn-ỉt.f*

V/25 ***snt*** [296/12]
Cairo, CG 20592 (Lange-Schäfer, *CGC* II, 232).

V/26 ***snt*** [296/12]
Leiden 3 (V 3) (Boeser, *Leiden* II, pl. 2).

V/27 ***snt*** [296/12]
TT 366 (Winlock, *Excavations at Deir el Bahar*, pl. 17/7).

V/28 ***snt*** [296/12]
Leiden 12 (V 85) (Boeser, *Leiden* II, pl. 11).

V/29 ***sn-nḫt*** [-]
Leiden 12 (V 85) (Boeser, *Leiden* II, pl. 11).

Son	*mʿnḫt*
Daughter	*sbt-ṯḫỉ*

V/30 ***ddt*** [403/5]
Leiden 11 (V 88) (Boeser, *Leiden* II, pl. 10).

V/31 ***ddt*** [403/5]
London, BM EA 572 (*HT* II, 22; ANOC 5/1).

V/32 ***ddt*** [403/5]

London, BM EA 571 (*HT* II, 16).

V/33 ***ddt*** [403/5]
Cairo, CG 20542 (Lange-Schäfer, *CGC* II 163-167).

V/34 ***ddt-mwt*** [403/11]
London, BM EA 213 (*HT* III, 5).

V/35 ***ddt-sbk*** [403/18]
Paris, Louvre C168 (ANOC 4/2).

V/36 /// ***mj***
Paris, Louvre C196 (Gayet, *Stèles de la XIIe dyn.*, pl. 59).

V/37 ?
Turin 1447 (Vasilika, *Museo Egizio*, no 13).

VI *wb3yt* (*wb3t*)

During the Middle Kingdom and Second Intermediate period the title *wb3* indicated a household servant connected with the preparation and serving of food.[189] W. Ward pointed out that Egyptian households of the Middle Kingdom often included servants with the title *wb3*, feminine *wb3t* or *wb3yt*;[190] they are frequently mentioned on the monuments, but we are not well informed about their very specific duties.[191] Women with this title are usually attested among servants and offering bearers.[192] However, female domestic servants did not constitute a uniform social rank; the variety of their titles perhaps suggests that each was associated with a different activity.

In P. Berlin P3033 the *wb3yt* was responsible for taking charge of the family's stores.[193] Thus, for W. Ward 'housekeeper' is perhaps a more adequate meaning of *wb3yt* in P. Berlin P3033, as well as in other cases.[194]

On the stela Louvre C 185, as well as on London, BM EA 162, a *wb3yt* presents a cup to the deceased.[195] It is important to note that *wb3yt*, as well as *wb3*, appears, on several of the stelae, among

---

[189] Gardiner, *AEO* I, 43*. See the Middle Kingdom stelae Leiden V 6 and London, BM EA 162.

[190] Ward, *Index MK*, 706; cf. Millard, *Position of Women in the Family and in Society*, 321-322.

[191] Helck, *Verwaltung*, 255ff; Ward, *The four Egyptian homographic roots*, 92-94.

[192] Ward, *Feminine Titles*, 6-7.

[193] Quirke, *Egyptian Literature*, 88-89.

[194] Ward, *Feminine Titles*, 7.

[195] However, Clère, (*RdÉ* 7, 1949, 23) notes that this is an exception since servant who performs this action, when named, is usually *wdpw*. It is worth of mentioning that this duty is frequently performed by *wb3* on other stelae. On the other hand, *wb3w* are attested among the gangs of mining and quarrying expeditions (Montet, *Ouâdi Hammâmât*, no 87; Goyon, *Ouadi Hammamat* no 64; Černy, *IS* nos 42, 94, 112, 114, 24, 105, 117, 106, 120).

household servants who do not perform specific duties. Furthermore, for Ward it *is evident that the wb3yt could also serve in temples* because *wb3* on the stela Cairo, CG 20380 carries the title "Master of the Household of Onuris".[196] However, most of the *wb3w* were, based on available data, concerned with the storage and preparation of food for the household. They were responsible for bringing the food from the preparation room to the place of eating, and with serving the food as well.[197] The *wb3w* attached to specific storehouses would be perhaps servants responsible for bringing supplies from the stores as needed.

When commenting on the titles of women attested on the offering tables from Lisht (four *iryt-ˁt,* five *wb3yt*, one *3ṯyt*, and one *ẖtt-pr*), Ward pointed out that *the importance of these women is not their unimposing titles, but rather where and whom they served*, as all of them *seem rather to be from the ranks of minor household servants. Precisely where and in what capacities these women served and why women with mediocre status should have owned such well-made offering tables will probably never be known.*[198]

However, it seems clear that *wb3yt* was the designation of women at work whose functions lay within the household. Within the range of household titles, we encounter the most difficulties in defining what a particular woman did or the extent, if any, of her authority.[199] Twenty titles (most are attendants of households) belong to the category of household titles, and just few of them are regular. The exact scope of their duties is almost impossible to determine. As H. G. Fischer observes: "the rank and status of such servants depended on the circumstances of their employer".[200] A good example of these

---

[196] Ward, *Feminine Titles*, 7. Cf. Bristol H 521 (Randall-Maciver - Mace, *El Amrah and Abydos*, 86, pl. 38).
n k3 n ẖkrt-nswt nb-ir /// m3ˁt-ḫrw mst n ***wb3yt ḥr*** *snb.tisi irt n 3ṯw n ṯt ḥḳ3 rn-snb m3ˁ-ḫrw*. It should be noted that designation *wb3yt* may also imply priestly duties, as is evident in case of its male counterpart. This can be explanation for the *wb3yt iw.f-n.i-r-psš* attested on the 'feminine stela' London, UC 14360 (Stefanović, *GM* 218, 2008, 90).

[197] Quirke, *Titles and Bureaux*, 66.

[198] Ward, in: *Women's Earliest Records*, 34-35.

[199] Ward, in: *Women's Earliest Records*, 34-35.

[200] Fischer, *Egyptian Studies* III, 76.

phenomena is the title *wb3yt* ('housemaid' or 'housekeeper'), because women with this title could have important duties on large estates or minor responsibilities in smaller households.[201]

According to O. D. Berlev the meaning of the term *wb3yt* is 'искусница' (mistress of household).[202] The main duty of *wb3yt* was food serving, but they were not responsible for preparing food; in cases where their hairdress tapers to a point from which a pigtail falls, as on stela New York, MMA 63.154, *wb3ywt* are serving liquids.[203] They may have other duties as well - the ladies from Lisht were court servants.

No matter what their duties, holders of the title *wb3yt* belonged to the group of *ḥmwt nswt* (servant women of the king). Berlev pointed out the offering table commissioned by the nomarch *sn-ꜥnḫ* where the members of his household have also been attested.[204] At the very end of the inscription field, the two servants are named: *ḥm nswt ḥḳ3-ỉn* and *wb3yt sḫ///*. According to Berlev, the term *wb3yt* is in this case an equivalent of the term *ḥm nswt* and in fact denotes a *ḥmt nswt*.[205]

The *wb3yt* attested on the stela Cairo, CG 20168 is highly intriguing. She is embracing the son of the main person on the stela (*wr mḏw šmꜥ mtỉ n s3*), 'as if she were his wife'.[206] For Berlev she is *ꜥnḫt*, concubine, of her master's son.[207] However, B.M. Bryan noted that *the tendency for household servants to become emotionally connected with the family members they served was as strong in Ancient Egypt as in Charlotte Bronte's or P.G. Wodehouse's*

---

201 Ward, in: *Women's Earliest Records*, 35-36.

202 Берлев, *Общественные отношения*, 297-301.

203 The girl on stela MMA 63.154 is labelled 'Asiatic' rather than 'servant'; however, the same individual wears a long wig on the Copenhagen stela, and bears a different designation – probably *wb3yt*. Compare with the appearance of the female servant (*ḥmt*) on stela Chicago, OIM 6739 (Teeter, *Ancient Egypt*, no 15, 38-39)

204 Petrie, *Courtiers*, pl. 25 (as well as Cairo, CG 20516, Petrie, *Courtiers*, pl. 12 and Paris, Louvre C 173).

205 Берлев, *Общественные отношения*, 299.

206 Берлев, *Общественные отношения*, 299-300.

207 Берлев, *Общественные отношения*, 301.

England.[208] As in case of stela Chicago, OIM 6739, stelae that show households, or groups of palace personnel, are not uncommon in the Late Middle Kingdom and Second Intermediate Period. It cannot always be determined whether the most prestigious person commissioned such a stela, or if it was made by the household staff that included their employer as a mark of respect. The fact that servants and their families are shown essentially in the same dress, position and size as a main person and his family, suggests that the staff may also have commissioned such stelae.[209]

However, this tells us nothing of the duties of the *wb3yt* though it does confirm their minor status as seen on funerary stelae. In the list of attestations that follows, sixty-three *wb3ywt* of the Middle Kingdom are recorded.[210] If we consider the members of the *wb3ywt* families, we can see that they are recorded (i.e. one of the parents and children) just in several cases. The husbands of *wb3ywt* are not attested at all.

VI/1 ***iw.f-n.i-r-psš*** [-]
London, UC 14360 (Stewart, *Petrie Collection*, no 139, pl. 34/2).
Mother *nbt-pr iw-n.*(*s*)*-snb*

VI/2 ***int-ḥꜥp(i)*** [36/5]
Cairo, GC 20022 (Lange-Schäfer, *CGC* I, 22-23).

VI/3 ***in-itf-snt*** [-]
Cairo, GC 20592 (Lange-Schäfer, *CGC* II, 230-232).

VI/4 ***isi*** [43/7]
Leiden 3 (V 3) (Boeser, *Leiden* II, Tf. 2).

[208] Bryan, in: *Mistress of the House, Mistress of Heaven: Women in Ancient Egypt*, 40.
[209] Teeter, *Ancient Egypt,* no 15, 38-39.
[210] Compare with O. D. Berlev's list of attestations (Берлев,*Общественные отношения*, 300; id. Берлев, *Трудовое население*, 325).

VI/5 ***iki*** [48/3][211]
Boston, MFA 1970.630 (Leprohon, *Stelae* I, 160-163).

VI/6 ***it-w3ḏt*** [49/6]
Pittsburgh 21538-38 (Petrie, *Courtiers*, 7; Patch, *Ancient Egypt*, no 18, 28-29; Quirke, *Titles and bureaux*, 134).

VI/7 ***iti*** [49/13]
Cairo, GC 20516 (Lange-Schäfer, *CGC* II, 108-111).

VI/8 ***ˁšm-mwt*** [71/21]
Tübingen 462 (ex Stuttgart 12.16; ANOC 60.2) (Spiegelberg-Pörtner, *AG* I, Tf. VIII/12; Brunner-Traut, *Sammlung der Universitat Tübingen*, 88-90, Tf. 10).

VI/9 ***bt3*** [99/4]
Paris, Louvre C 185 (E 3122) (Gayet, *Stèles de la XIIe dyn.*, pl. 48 [11-12]).

VI/10 ***mry*** [160/1]
Cairo, GC 20398 (Lange-Schäfer, *CGC* I, 396-397).

VI/11 ***mrryt*** [162/25]
Leiden 33 (V 102) (Boeser, *Leiden* II, Tf. XXI).

VI/12 ***nb-ḥr-k3w*** [191/24]
Cairo, GC 20168 (Lange-Schäfer, *CGC* I, 199-200).

VI/13 ***nbt-pt*** [-]
London, BM EA 152 (*HT* II, 34; Freed, in: *Studies Simpson* I, 313).

VI/14 ***nbt-ḥtp*** [189/7]
Cairo, GC 20649 (Lange-Schäfer, *CGC* II, 283-284).

---

[211] She is the one of the *wb3ywt nt ḥry n tm it.f-sn* (the female butlers of the *ḥry n tm it.f-sn*).

VI/15 ***nfr-iw*** [194/7]
Cairo, GC 20119 (Lange-Schäfer, *CGC* I, 267).

VI/16 ***nfr-iw*** [194/7]
Cairo, GC 20441 (Lange-Schäfer, *CGC* II, 39).

VI/17 ***nḥ(w)*** [207/19]
Moscow 1136 (Hodjash - Berlev, *Pushkin Museum*, no 40).

VI/18 ***nẖt*** [209/16]
Cairo, GC 20098 (Lange-Schäfer, *CGC* I, 119-120).

VI/19 ***nẖt*** ? [209/16]
Cairo, GC 20722 (Lange-Schäfer, *CGC* II, 349-352).

VI/20 ***nẖti*** [212/1]
Cairo, GC 23029 (JdE 31146) (Kamal, *Tables d'offrandes*, 24, pl. XIII).

**im3ẖt rẖ(t) nsw*

Mother *s3t-sbk.i*

VI/21*rꜥ///*
Chicago, OIM 6740 (Garstang, *El-Arabah*, 35, pl. XIII/5).

VI/22 ***rn.s-snb*** [224/1]
Cairo, GC 20119 (Lange-Schäfer, *CGC* I, 267).

VI/23 ***rnpt-nfr*** [224/11]
Cairo, JdE 63947 (Arnold, *Complex of Senwosret* I, pl. 80, no 120).

Father *byt* ?

VI/24 ***ḥnwt*** [242/15][212]
Boston, MFA 1970.630 (Leprohon, *Stelae* I, 160-163).

VI/25 ***ḥnwt*** [242/18][213]

---

[212] Probably in service of the *imy-ẖt s3w-pr imny*.

Boston, MFA 1970.630 (Leprohon, *Stelae* I, 160-163).

VI/26 ***ḥtpt*** [250/13][214]
Paris, Louvre C 303 (C 247; E 3467) (Habachi, *Elephantine* IV, 167-168; pl. 211a).
Mother *s3t-ḥtḥr*

VI/27 ***ḥḳ3.wn*** [256/7]
Cairo, GC 23049 (JdE 31154) (Kamal, *Tables d'offrandes*, 24, pl. XIII).
**im3ḫt rḫ(t) nsw*
Mother *s3t-sbk*

VI/28 ***ḥḳ3-snb*** [256/16]
Cairo, GC 23051 (JdE 31153) (Kamal, *Tables d'offrandes*, 24, pl. XIII).
**im3ḫyt rḫ(t) nsw mrt ist*
Mother *s3t-w3ḏit*

VI/29 ***ḥtp*** [257/22]
London, BM EA 571 (*HT* II, 16).

VI/30 ***ḥtpt*** [260/13]
TT 60 (Davies, *Antefoker*, pl. 26).

VI/31 ***ẖty*** [277/26]
Cairo, GC 20098 (Lange-Schäfer, *CGC* I, 119-120).

VI/32 ***s3t-ipi-ktt*** [285/24]
Cairo, GC 20736 (Lange-Schäfer, *CGC* II, 367).

VI/33 ***s3t-itf*** [287/10]
Cairo, GC 20098 (Lange-Schäfer, *CGC* I, 119-120).

---

[213] She is the one of the *wb3ywt nt ḥry n tm it.f-sn* (the female butlers of the *ḥry n tm it.f-sn*).
[214] *wb3yt.f* (*mr mšʿ sḥtp-ib*) *ḥst.f.* Contra Habachi's reading: *His favoured daughter Hetepet, born of Sathator* (*Elephantine* IV, 168).

VI/34 ***s3t-imn*** [286/6]
Cairo, GC 20561 (ANOC 4; Lange-Schäfer, *CGC* II, 194-196).

VI/35 ***s3t-ꜥnḫw*** [287/18]
Cairo, GC 23064 (Gautier-Jequier, *Fouilles de Licht*, 58, fig. 61).
**im3ḫ(t) rḫt nswt*
Mother *iy*

VI/36 ***s3t-ꜥnḫ.tisi*** [287/19]
Cairo, GC 20098 (Lange-Schäfer, *CGC* I, 119-120).

VI/37 ***s3t-b3stt*** [288/11]
Turin 1626 (1534) (Maspero, *RT* 3, 1882, 115-117, no 107).

VI/38 ***s3t-mnw*** [289/5]
Oxford, Ashmolian 1922.143 (Petrie, *Courtiers*, pl. 12/7).
Daughter *sddt*

VI/39 ***s3t-mnw*** [289/5]
Cairo, GC 20024 (Lange-Schäfer, *CGC* I, 26-29).

VI/40 ***s3t-rꜥ*** [290/21]
Fitzwilliam Museum, Cambridge E.SS.16 (Martin, *Fitzwilliam Museum*, 37 [23]).

VI/41 ***s3t-ḥtḥr*** [291/14]
Cairo, GC 23062 (Gautier-Jequier, *Fouilles de Licht*, 57, fig. 60).
**im3ḫ(t) rḫt nswt*
Mother *snt*

VI/42 ***s3t-ḥri-ib*** [292/4]
Cairo, GC 20516 (Lange-Schäfer, *CGC* II, 108-111).

VI/43 ***s3t-ḫnti-ẖty*** [292/21]
London, BM EA 162 (*HT* IV, 33; ANOC 2.3).

VI/44 ***s3t-k3-iwnw*** [294/7]

1) New York, MMA 63.154 (Fischer, *Egyptian Studies* III, 130-133; ANOC 59.1).
2) Ny Carlsberg, AEIN 964 (Koefoed-Petersen, *Stele eg. Copenhague,* 16; ANOC 59.2).

VI/45 ***sbk-nḫt* / *ꜥnḫt.sy*** [304/15] / [68/23]
Cairo, GC 20022 (Lange-Schäfer, *CGC* I, 22-23).

VI/46 ***sn-ꜥnḫ*** [308/14]
London, BM EA 213 (*HT* III, 5).

VI/47 ***snb*** [312/15]
Musées Royaux d'Art er d'Historie, Bruxelles E 2149 (Černy, *IS*, no 153, pl. XL).

VI/48 ***snb-rn-snbw*** [-]
1) New York, MMA 63.154 (Fischer, *Egyptian Studies* III, 130-133; ANOC 59.1).
2) Ny Carlsberg, AEIN 964 (Koefoed-Petersen, *Stele eg. Copenhague,* 16; ANOC 59.2).
**ꜥꜣmt*

VI/49 ***snb-ddi*** [-]
New York, MMA 69.30 (Fischer, *Egyptian Studies* III, 125, pl. 21).

VI/50 ***snt*** ? [296/21]
Cairo, GC 20098 (Lange-Schäfer, *CGC* I, 119-120).

VI/51 ***šdj-jnj-ḥrjt*** [332/1]
Chicago, OIM 6740 (Garstang, *El-Arabah*, 35, pl. XIII/5).

VI/52 ***gm.s*** [352/2]
Cairo, GC 20119 (Lange-Schäfer, *CGC* I, 267).

VI/53 ***tit*** [378/19]
Oxford, Ashmolian 1922.143 (Petrie, *Courtiers*, pl. 12/7).

VI/54 ***ṯꜣt*** [389/14]

Cairo, GC 20398 (Lange-Schäfer, *CGC* I, 396-397).

VI/55 *ḏdw-sbk* ? [402/24]
London, BM EA 1322 (*HT* III, 33).

VI/56 *ddt-mwt* [403/11]
Cairo, GC 20323 (Lange-Schäfer, *CGC* I, 336).

VI/57 *ddt-sbk* [403/18]
London, BM EA 213 (*HT* III, 5).

VI/58 *ddt-sbk* [403/18]
Cairo, GC 20022 (Lange-Schäfer, *CGC* I, 22-23).

VI/59 *ḏꜣꜥr* [-]
Paris, Louvre C 173 (Gayet, *Stèles de la XIIe dyn.*, pl. 29).
Mother *mmi* (?)

VI/60 *sẖ*///
Museum of Faculty of Letters, Kyoto University (Petrie, *Courtiers*, pl. 23/2, 25).

VI/61 ///*ḥtp*
TT 60 (Davies, *Antefoker*, pl. 26).

VI/62 ///*tꜣ*
Cairo, GC 20499 (Lange-Schäfer, *CGC* II, 90-91).

VI/63 ///
Aswan, Tomb no 28 (*Dem*, 152).

VII *b3kt nt ḥḳ3*

W. Ward pointed out that women with the title *b3kt nt ḥḳ3* were usually married to minor functionaries. According to his research, "the ruler is probably a local nomarch or other official rather than the king so that these women held positions in provincial courts."[215] G. Robins also noted that *b3kwt nwt ḥḳ3* usually mark women married to the minor functionaries. In this case *ḥḳ3* probably refers to a *provincial governor rather than the king, so this would not be a position held in capital.*[216] However, it is possible that the *b3kwt nwt ḥḳ3*, as well as the *ẖkrwt-nswt* and *ʿnḫwt nwt nswt tpwt*, belong to the social stratum close to the king's court and administration.[217] On the other hand, the title could also be an honorific designation, i.e. rank title, without any implications of 'real duties'.

In the list of attestations that follows, thirty-five *b3kwt nwt ḥḳ3* of the Middle Kingdom and Second Intermediate Period are recorded. Among the male members of the *b3kwt nwt ḥḳ3* families the most prominent place belongs to the holders of the titles of *wr mḏw šmʿ* and *s3b r nḫn*. The high number of *s3b r nḫn*, officials attached to the office of the vizier,[218] may demonstrate their closeness to the court circles, or royal household.

Title	Husband	Son
wr mḏw šmʿ		
ḥry-ḥb		
šmsw		

[215] Ward, *Index MK*, 778; Ward, *Feminine titles*, 7; Millard, *Position of Women in the Family and in Society*, 273-274.
cf. Franke, *JEA* 76, 1990, 229.
[216] Robins, *Women in Ancient Egypt*, 115.
[217] Franke, *JEA* 76, 1990, 229. See also Trapani, in: *Proceedings of the Ninth International Congress of Egyptologists*, 1833.
[218] Quirke, *Titles and bureaux*, 89-90.

rḫ nswt m3ʿ		
ḥm-nṯr n ḥr bhdt		
rḫ nswt mr ḥsw		
ḥry ntm		
s3b r nḫn		
imy-ḫt		
Unspecified		

The designation 'Great one of the Southern Ten' was, as D. Franke suggested, an explanatory title ('Beititel').[219] Their holders belonged to the circle of the late Middle Kingdom court society, as well as the *b3kwt nwt ḥk3*, fulfilling various task as representatives of central administration. As in the case of other feminine titles, the lack of information concerning the parental background of *b3kwt nwt ḥk3* does not allow us to make even a suggestion of their before-marriage social standing. However, judging from the titles of their daughters, it is worth of noting that none of them 'inherited the title of their mother'.

ẖkrt-nswt	*ʿnḫt nt tpt nswt*	*nbt-pr*
3	2	1

The title *b3kt nt ḥk3* is never associated with another title; no other rank or administrative titles are recorded with the titulary of 'female servant of the ruler'. It is possible that the title *b3kt nt ḥk3* belongs to the same category as the title *wr mḏw šmʿ*, i.e., an explanatory title.

VII/1 *3b-m33* [-]
(Martin, *MDAIK* 35, 1975, 223, no 70).

VII/2 *iy* [7/17]
Cairo, CG 20742 (Lange-Schäfer, *CGC* II, 373-376).
Mother *s3t-b3stt*

[219] Franke, in: *Studies Assman*, 123.

VII/3 ***iw-n.s-it.s*** [13/24][220]
Copenhagen, Nationalmuseet, B.2 (Mogensen, *Inscriptions Copenhague*, 14-15, pl. XIII).
Husband *wr mḏw šmꜥ wsr*

VII/4 ***imny*** [31/13]
Cairo, JdE 75168 (Martin, *Seals*, 203).

VII/5 ***im-ḏd*** [-]
Clandeboye Collection 6 (Edwards, *JEA* 51, 1965, 27/6).[221]
Husband *wr mḏw šmꜥ iw////ḥtp* (?)

VII/6 ***wꜣḏt*** [74/29]
Berkeley CA, Phoebe Apperson Hearst Museum of Anthropology, 6.19888 (Lutz, *Tomb Steles*, no 80).
Daughter *ẖkrt-nswt mwt.i-snb.ti*

VII/7 ***bꜣkit*** [93/3]
London, BM EA 30524 (Martin, *Seals*, 443).

VII/8 ***bbi*** [95/16]
Cairo, JdE 75164 (Martin, *Seals*, 447).

VII/9 ***ptḥ-nfr*** [140/14]
Florence 7603 (Bostico, *Le Stele Egiz.*, no 43, 46-47).
Husband *ḥry-ḥb snb.wi*
Son (?) *wr mḏw šmꜥ nn-rs*

VII/10 ***mi*** ? [-]
(Martin, *Seals*, 1906).

VII/11 ***mwt-pw-snb*** ? [-]
Bolton 1920.10.12 (ex 10.20.12) (Stefanović, *SAK* 2009).

---

[220] Another woman with the same, rare name is attested on London, BM EA 197 (*HT* IV, 46).
[221] Cf. Ward, *Feminine Titles*, 7, and Franke, *JEA* 76, 1990, 229.

Husband	*šmsw ddi*
Sons ?	*rḫ nswt m3ʿ rn-snb*
	wr mdw šmʿ nb-swmnw
	wr mdw šmʿ rs-snb
	wr mdw šmʿ rn-snb
Daughters ?	*nbt-pr nfr-ḥtp*
	ʿnḫt nt nswt tpt nfr-ḥtp
	ʿnḫt nt nswt tpt mwt-p(w)-snb

VII/12 *mrwt* [162/14]
Chicago, OIM 18572 (Martin, *Seals*, 618).

VII/13 *nbw-m-s3* [191/7]
(Alliot, *Tell Edfou*, 33, pl. 17/2, no 13).

Husband	*smswh3yt ḥrw-ʿ3*[222]

VII/14 *nbw-n-rḫwt* [191/11]
Berlin 4423 (*AIB I*, 150).

VII/15 *nfrw* [206/16]
Brooklyn NY, Brooklyn Museum of Fine Arts, 37.1349E (James, *Corpus of Hieroglyphic Inscriptions* I, 45-6 [104c] pl. lxxxviii).

VII/16 *nḥ* [207/9]
London, BM EA 42746 (Martin, *Seals*, 759).

VII/17 *rn.s-rs* [223/23]
1) Cairo, CG 20481 (Lange-Schäfer, *CGC* II, 76-77).
2) Cairo, CG 20743[223] (Lange-Schäfer, *CGC* II, 376-377).

Husband ?	*wr mdw šmʿ ddw-sbk*

VII/18 *ḥtpt* [260/13]
Boston, MFA 72.766 (Leprohon, *Stelae* I, 1-3).

Husband	*wr mdw šmʿ sbk-(ḥ)tp*
Son	*rḫ nswt mr ḥsw ḫmi*

---

[222] Cf. Franke, *Doss.*, 428.
[223] Maspero, *ZÄS* 20, 1882, 122-123.

VII/19 *ḫmm* [269/21]
Cairo, CG 20086 (Lange-Schäfer, *CGC* I, 101-103).
Husband ?[224]

VII/20 *ḫnsw* [270/16]
(Winlock, *The Rise and Fall*, p. 72, pl. 39/III; Id., *AJSLL* 57/2, 1940, 156, fig. 14).

VII/21 *s3t-ptḥ* [288/22]
(Martin, *Seals*, 1355).

VII/22 *s3t///*
Cairo, CG 20673 (Lange-Schäfer, *CGC II*, 300-301).
Husband *ỉmn-ʿ3*
Son *wr mḏw šmʿ sbm-m-s3.f*

VII/23 *s3t-nḫt* [290/14]
Cairo, JdE 51349 (Martin, *Seals*, 1357).

VII/24 *s3t-ḥtḥt* [291/14]
1) London, BM EA 30866 (Petrie - Mace, *Diospolis Parva*, pl. 27, p. 53).
2) Chicago, OIM 5518 (Petrie - Mace, *Diospolis Parva*, pl. 27, p. 53; *The Life of Meresamun*, no 3, 35).

VII/25 *snnw* [310/21]
(Winlock, *The Rise and Fall*, p. 72, pl. 39/III; Id., *AJSLL* 57/2, 1940, 156, fig. 14).
Husband *s3b r nḫn nṯr-ỉsỉ*

VII/26 *t3-ḥnwt* [365/19]

---

[224] For the main person on the monument see Grajetzki, *Zentralverwaltung,* 187, and Franke, in: *Studies Assman*, 99.

Cairo, CG 20530 (Lange-Schäfer, *CCG* II, 131-135; Trapani, in: *Proceedings of the Ninth International Congress of Egyptologists,* 1827-1838).

Daughter *ẖkrt-nswt nbw-ḫʿi.s*

VII/27 ***di-n-nbt*** ? [397/2]

Paris, Louvre C 193 (E 3294) (Gayet, *Stèles de la XIIe dyn.*, pl. 50).

Husband *imy-ḫt ʿ3*

Son *wr mḏw šmʿ rn-snb*

VII/28 ***di-n-sn*** [-]

London, BM EA 1348 (*HT* IV, 27; Bourriau, *Pharaohs and Mortals*, 57-59, no 45).

VII/29 ***dtt*** [400/27]

New York, MMA 21.2.68 (Hayes, *The Scepter of Egypt* I, 346, fig. 227 [upper right]).

Husband ? *wr mḏw šmʿ 3w-rs*

VII/30 ***ddt*** [403/5]

Sotheby Sale Cat. (Amherst), June 13-17, 1921, no 450 (*Catalogue of the Amherst Collection*). *[13–17 June, 1921]* (London, 1921).

VII/31 ///

Private Collection, Tadross (Vernus, *RdÉ* 26, 1974, 101-114).

Husband *wr mḏw šmʿ snb(.n)-r-3w*

Sons *s3b r nḫn sbk-m-ḥb*

wr mḏw šmʿ ʿnḫ-pw-ptḥ

wr mḏw šmʿ snbw

s3b r nḫn ḥmn-ḫwi.f

s3b r nḫn ii-wi-ptḥ

ḥry n tm rdi-n-ptḥ

VII/32 ///

Cairo, JdE 42824 (*PM* 1:2, 619).

VII/33 ///

Moscow 2174 (Martin, *Seals*, 1807).

VII/34 ///
Shalfak 31-3-200 [B 7686] (Dunham - Janssen, *SCF II*, pl. 61B).

VII/35 ///
Shalfak 31-3-200 [B 7686] (Dunham - Janssen, *SCF II*, pl. 61B).

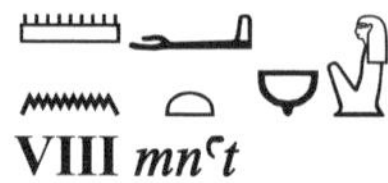

VIII *mnꜥt*

One of the titles of women engaged in the private households was *mnꜥt*.[225] The title *mnꜥt* refers to the wet nurse or nanny. In two letters from Lahun as well as in P. Boulaq 18, the 'house of nurses' is also attested.[226] Since the term *mnꜥt*, determined with the sign for breast, is used both for the nurse herself and the house of nurses, as well as in cases where the title is used for men, it perhaps indicates a person who had a broader role in the rising of a child or young person.[227]

During the Middle Kingdom and Second Intermediate Period *mnꜥwt* were recorded among the members of the family of their 'protégé' and quite often recorded as *mnꜥt.f /.s* on stelae and other monuments, specifying the special role they played in the daily life of the family. For example, in the Late Middle Kingdom / Second Intermediate Period tomb of Bebi at Elkab, one scene shows the owner opposite his children while behind each of them a nurse (*mnꜥt*)

---

[225] The *mnꜥ / mnꜥt* is one of the terms for nurse or tutor (not attested as title during the Old Kingdom). Cf. Jones, *Index of Ancient Egyptian Titles*, no 1605; Hannig, *Ägyptisches Wörterbuch* II, 1073-1074; Ward, *Feminine Titles*, 23; Id., *Index MK*, 799; Millard, *Position of Women in the Family and in Society*, 310-314; Roehrig, in: *Mistress of the House, Mistress of Heaven: Women in Ancient Egypt*, 16-19; Szpakowska, *Daily Life in Ancient Egyp*, 35-37; Stefanović, *GM* 216, 2008, 79-90, no 8; Burt, *BIFAO* 107, 2008, 109-126. For the *mnꜥt* as part of epithets, see Doxey, *Non-royal Epithets*, 303.

[226] For the Middle Kingdom term (*rmṯ*) *pr mnꜥt / pr mnꜥw* see: MMA 35.5.55 (Hayes, *JEA* 33, 1947, 2); P. Boulaq 18 (Scharff, *ZÄS* 57, 1922, Tf. 17/58; Tf 12/41; Tf. 9/30; Tf. 8/25; Tf. 7/21; Tf. 6/18; Tf. 5/12; Tf. 2/7); London, UC 32124 and UC 32216 (Collier-Quirke, *The UCL Lahun Papyri: Letters*, 58-61, 152-155). Cf. Quirke, *The Administration of Egypt*, 40, 96; Spalinger, *SAK* 12, 1985, 190, n. 8; Szpakowska, *Daily Life in Ancient Egypt*, 35.

[227] Feucht, *Das Kind im Alten Ägypten*, 285; cf. Markoe - Capel, *Mistress of the House, Mistress of Heaven*, 59-62; Robins, *Women in Ancient Egypt*, 88-91.

is standing.[228] On stela Oxford, QC 1113 a *mnʿt* stands behind the man who dedicated the stela, with her hand on his shoulder.[229] For W. Ward she was *evidently a much-loved servant who had raised the boy from infancy, hence more a nanny than a nurse.*[230]

Through their milk, they become related to the child and to his family. Thus, on the stela Cairo, CG 20457 the son of the nurse was 'Milchbruder' of the main person on the monument.[231] In not so few cases, the members of the families of the nurses can be found represented on the stelae of their employers.[232] The husband of *mnʿt* is perhaps recorded on the stela Munich 8 (Gl WAF 34) where she sits opposite the main person of the monument, the *iry pḏt nfr-nꜣ-ii.*[233] Millard notes that husbands of many of the nurses may be concealed among the other people named on the stelae or in tombs, and that *there is no reason to assume that the nurses were unmarried mothers, perhaps concubines of the fathers of their foster-children, though this may have happened occasionally.*[234] However, it is important to note that even when their children are mentioned, they are labelled, as a rule, as *sꜣ / sꜣt.s*. Their offspring were probably raised together with the children who were in the care of the nurse.

In the list of attestations that follows, ninety-three Middle Kingdom and Second Intermediate Period holders of the title *mnʿt* are recorded.[235]

---

[228] *LD* Text IV, 52-53; Wildung, *Sesostris und Amenemhat*, 95, fig. 85 (wrongly noted as Sebeknakht's tomb; cf. Stefanović, *GM* 215, 2008, 79). For the ritual meaning of the scene see Altenmüller, *Welt des Orients* 14, 1983, 30-45; Willems, *Coffin of Heqata*, 131, n. 586; Vasiljević, *SAK-Beihefte* 9, 2003, 435. See also Newberry, *Beni Hasan* I, pl. 35.

[229] Smither – Dakin, *JEA* 25, 1939, 163-165.

[230] Ward, *Feminine Titles*, 8.

[231] *in sn.f n mnʿ isi mꜣʿ-ḫrw sʿnḫ rn.f* Cf. D. Franke, *AVB*, 360, 102.

[232] Cf. VIII/32.

[233] Franke, *Doss.*, no 309; Stefanović, *Military Titles*, no 919.

[234] Millard, *Position of Women in the Family and in Society*, 311-312.

[235] See: Millard, *Position of Women in the Family and in Society*, 310-311. The title on the stela Liverpool 1977.109.36 is uncertain. See Ogdon, *RSUE* 19, 2002, 7-12, and Schneider, *Ausländer in Ägypten* II, 285.

VIII/1 *ꜣst* [3/18]
London, BM EA 143 (*HT* II, pl. 44).

VIII/2 *ỉỉỉ* [7/17]
Wien, KHM ÄS 110 (Hein – Satzinger, *Stelen des Mittleren Reiches I*, 26-29).

VIII/3 *ỉỉỉ* [8/8]
London, UC 32216 (Collier-Quirke, *The UCL Lahun Papyri: Letters*, 152-155).

VIII/4 *ỉỉ-m-ḥtp* [9/2]
Aswan 1308 (Habachi, *Elephantine* IV, no 93, p. 107).

VIII/5 *ỉỉw-snb* [11/7]
Cairo, CG 20289 (Lange - Schäfer, *CGC* I, 303-4).

VIII/6 *ỉỉtỉ* [-]
Wien, KHM ÄS 204 (Hein – Satzinger, *Stelen des Mittleren Reiches* I, 162-167).

VIII/7 *ỉb(.ỉ)-ỉʿ(w)* [19/4]
Cairo, CG 20426 (Lange - Schäfer, *CGC* II, 21-2).
**sꜣ-ỉmn mst.n bb mnʿt.f ib(.ỉ)-ỉʿ(w)*

VIII/8 *ỉb(.ỉ)-ỉʿ(.w)* [19/4]
Chicago, OIM 6740 (Garstang, *El-Arabah*, 35, pl. XIII/5 [= E 172]).
Son *ỉmn-ḥtp*

VIII/9 *ỉb.ỉ-ḫnỉỉ* [-]
(Franke, *Heqaib*, 87, Tf. 9).
**ẖkrt-nsw nbw-r-mnỉ //// mnʿt.s ib.ỉ-ḫnỉỉ*

VIII/10 *ỉpw* [23/3]
Elkab, Tomb 8bis (*LD* Text IV, 53).
**///sbk-nḫt mnʿt.f ỉpw*

VIII/11 *ỉpwỉ* [23/24]

Wien, KHM ÄS 180 (Hein – Satzinger, *Stelen des Mittleren Reiches* II, 103-111).[236]

Daughter *nfrt-iw*

VIII/12 *in* [32/19]

Cairo, CG 20352 (Lange - Schäfer, *CGC* I, 363).

Son *iwii*

VIII/13 *irti.t*[237] [42/19]

(Newberry, *PSBA* 25, 1903, 135-136; Ball, *Light From the East*, 76-77).

VIII/14 *it* [49/7]

Cairo, CG 20516 (Lange - Schäfer, *CGC* II, 108-111).

**ẖry-ḥb ḥtp ms.n ḥtpt /////// mnʿt.f it*

Mother *iti*

VIII/15 *iti* [49/15]

Cairo, CG 20581 (Lange - Schäfer, *CGC* II, 221-222).

Mother *mnt*

VIII/16 *iti* [50/3]

Paris, Louvre C 249 (E 8023) (Andreu, *BIFAO* 80, 1980, 139-147, pl. xxxviii-xxxix).

Mother *mwt.s*

VIII/17 *ʿ3mt* [59/3][238]

---

236 The family of *mnʿt ipwi* according to Hein – Satzinger, *Stelen des Mittleren Reiches* II, 106.

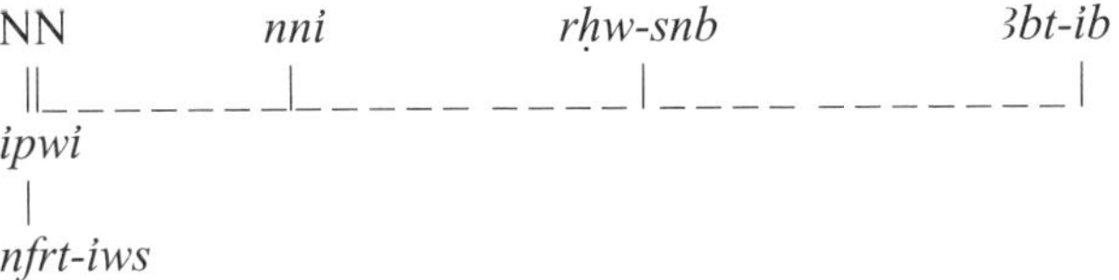

237 Uncertain reading.

238 Schneider, *Ausländer in Ägypten* II, 285.

Oxford, QC 1111 (Smither – Dakin, *JEA* 25, 1939, 159-160, no 2; ANOC 63.1).

VIII/18 ***ꜥnḫ*** [62/19]
Cairo, CG 20644 (Lange - Schäfer, *CGC* II, 281).

VIII/19 ***ꜥndit*** [70/11]
Sale Cat. (Amherst), June 13-17, 1921, no 445 (*Catalogue of the Amherst Collection*).

VIII/20 ***wꜣḏ.w(t)*** [75/17]
London, BM EA 831 (*HT* IV, pl. 12).
**iry-ꜥt wdpw /// mnꜥt.f wꜣḏ.w(t)*
Mother *mꜥmꜥw*

VIII/21 ***wii*** [76/5]
Paris, Louvre C 249 (E 8023) (Andreu, *BIFAO* 80, 1980, 139- 147, pl. xxxviii-xxxix).
Mother *irt.n mwt.s*

VIII/22 ***bbi*** [95/16]
Aswan 1308 (Habachi, *Elephantine* IV, no 93, p. 107).

VIII/23 ***bnrt*** [97/17]
Chiddingston Castle, EDECC:01.2882 (Grajetzki, in: in: *IBAES* V, 62-65).

VIII/24 ***ppw*** [132/14]
Turin 1626 (1534) (Maspero, *RT* 3, 1882, 115-117, no 107).
**ꜥb-kꜣw ///// mnꜥt.f ppw*

VIII/25 ***psšw*** [137/7]
Cairo, CG 20426 (Lange - Schäfer, *CGC* II, 21-2).
**ḫnsw ///// mnꜥt.s psšw*

VIII/26 ***mw-nw-ib*** [147/1]
Marseille 28 (Maspero, *RT* 13, 1890, 117).

VIII/27 ***mwt-n.s*** [-]
Cairo, JdE 55618 (Abdalla, *JEA* 78, 1992, 99-101, fig. 4, pl. XXI).
**mwt-m-sꜣ.s ///// mnꜥt.s mwt-n.s*

VIII/28 ***mmi*** [149/18]
Cairo, CG 20724 (Lange - Schäfer, *CGC* II, 353-355).

VIII/29 ***mnw-ꜥꜣ*** [151/17]
Cairo, CG 20540 (Lange - Schäfer, *CGC* II, 158-161).

VIII/30 ***msyt*** [165/10]
Cairo, CG 20540 (Lange - Schäfer, *CGC* II, 158-161).

VIII/31 ***mḏḥw*** [168/8]
Leiden 48 (V 101) (Boeser, *Leiden* II, Tf. 37).
Mother *irt.n mwt.s*

VIII/32 ***nb-idr-n-ḫꜣ*** [183/22]
Munich 8 (Gl WAF 34) (Dyroff-Pörtner, *AG* II, Tf. V; ANOC 44.1).
Husband (?) *iry-pḏt nfr-nꜣ-ii*

VIII/33 ***nb.i-m-wiꜣ*** [184/22]
Cairo, CG 20742 (Lange - Schäfer, *CGC* II, 373-377).

VIII/34 ***nbt-itf*** [188/7]
Elkab, Tomb 8bis (*LD* Text IV, 52).
**//// mnꜥt.f nbt-itf*

VIII/35 ***nbw*** ? [190/3]
Elkab, Tomb 8bis (*LD* Text IV, 53).
**///ii-mr mnꜥt.f nbw* (?)

VIII/36 ***nb-m-ḥb*** [191/5]
Elkab, Tomb 8bis (*LD* Text IV, 52).

VIII/37 ***nb-ḥr-š.s*** [191/23]
Elkab, Tomb 8bis (*LD* Text IV, 53).
**///nfr-ḥtp mnꜥt.f nb-ḥr-š.s*

VIII/38 ***nfr-tm*** [200/24]
Cairo, CG 20742 (Lange - Schäfer, *CGC* II, 373-377).

VIII/39 ***nfr.iit*** [203/15]
Cairo, CG 20580 (Lange - Schäfer, *CGC* II, 219-220).

VIII/40 ***nni*** [205/9]
Elkab, Tomb 8bis (*LD* Text IV, 53)
**///sbk-nḫt mnʿt.f nni*

VIII/41 ***nni*** [205/9]
Elkab, Tomb 8bis (*LD* Text V, 54).
**///ẖkrt-nswt nfrt-wbn.s mnʿt.s nni*

VIII/42 ***nḫt*** [209/16]
Marseille 24 (Maspero, *RT* 13, 1890, 114-115).

VIII/43 ***nt-ḥḏ*** [-]
London, UC 32143A (Collier - Quirke, *The UCL Lahun Papyri: Accounts*, 176-177).

VIII/44 ***rn-snb*** [222/26]
Paris, Louvre E 20164 (ex Museé Guimet C14) (Moret, *Annales du Musee Guimet*, 31-34, pl. XIII/14).

VIII/45 ***rn-snb-ktty*** [-]
(Habachi, *Elephantine* IV, no 90, p. 105).

VIII/46 ***rn.f-ʿnḫ*** [223/6]
Manchester 3306 (Garstang, *El-Arabah*, pl. IV/V).[239]
Mother *ddi*

VIII/47 ***rn.s-snb*** [224/1]
(Petrie, *Season*, no 137).
* //// *mnʿt.s rn.s-snb*

---

[239] *mnʿt nt ib.f* "the nurse of his heart".

Mother ////iry-pw

VIII/48 ***rḫw-twt*** [225/27]
1) Cairo, CG 20426 (Lange - Schäfer, *CGC* II, 21-2).
2) Washington, Smithsonian Museum (Peet, *Cem. Abydos*, pl. 14/2, p. 36).

**nb-swmnw mnˁt.f rḫw-twt*[240]

VIII/49 ***rḫw-twt*** [226/1]
Cambridge, Fitzwilliam Museum E 9.1922 (Petrie, *Courtiers*, pls. 22.1, 23.1).

VIII/50 ***ḥpw*** [238/14]
Cairo, CG 20057 (Lange - Schäfer, *CGC* I, 68-71).

Mother *ˁbt-kꜣ.wt*

VIII/51 ***ḥpw*** [238/14]
London, BM EA 129 (*HT* II, pl. 41-43).

VIII/52 ***ḥpw*** [238/14]
London, BM EA 129 (*HT* II, pl. 41-43).

Mother *iii*

VIII/53 ***ḥp.ii.w*** [238/9]
Cairo, CG 20018 (Lange - Schäfer, *CGC* I, 17-18).

Daughter *nbt-pr bb*

VIII/54 ***ḥmt*** [240/10]
Cairo, CG 20441 (Lange - Schäfer, *CGC* II, 39).

VIII/55 ***ḥnwt*** [242/18]
Aswan 1356 (Habachi, *Elephantine* IV, no 85, p. 102).

VIII/56 ***ḥnt*** [-]
Saint-Omer, Musée de l'Hôtel Sandelin 6282 (*Les Cultes Funéraires en Égypte et en Nubie*, no 5).

---

[240] Franke, *AVB*, 360; cf. Franke, *Doss.*, no 302.

VIII/57 ***ḥḳi*** [255/24]
Wien, KHM ÄS 110 (Hein – Satzinger, *Stelen des Mittleren Reiches* I, 26-29).

VIII/58 ***ḥtp*** [257/22]
(Petrie, *Season*, no 286).
Mother *ḥtp.i*

VIII/59 ***ḥtpt*** [260/13][241]
(Frankfort, *JEA* 14, 1928, 240-241, no. 6, pl. XX/1, fig. 2).
Son *iry-ʿt n ʿḥ s-n-wsrt*

VIII/60 ***ẖwi*** [265/26]
Lisht-north, Anonymous tomb (Arnold, *Tomb Architecture at Lisht*, 86-87, pl. 169).
**/// mnʿt.f mrt.f ẖwi*

VIII/61 ***ẖtrwi*** [-]
Bani Hasan, Tomb 3 (Newberry, *Beni Hasan* I, pl. 35).

VIII/62 ***s3(t)-imn*** [286/6]
Cairo, CG 20436 (Lange - Schäfer, *CGC* II, 33-35).

VIII/63 ***s3t-imn*** [286/6]
Marseille 24 (Maspero, *RT* 13, 1890, 114-115).

VIII/64 ***s3t-bbi*** [288/13]
Cairo, CG 20607 (Lange - Schäfer, *CGC* II, 246).
**ẖtmty n šmsw m-s3.f ////// mnʿt.f s3t-bbi*

VIII/65 ***s3t-nfr*** [290/11]
1) (Petrie, *Season*, no 74).
2) (Petrie, *Season*, no 106).
Mother *iby*

[241] Cf. Ranke, *PN* II, 289/25.

VIII/66 ***s3t-nn-rn.f*** [290/13]
Paris, Louvre C 168 (Gayet, *Stèles de la XIIe dyn.*, pl. 56).

VIII/67 ***s3t-rnn-wtt*** [290/23]
Florence 2564 (Bosticco, *Le stele egiz.*, no 37, p. 41-42).
Mother *ẖrt-k3*

VIII/68 ***s3t-rns.i*** [291/1]
Paris, Louvre C 168 (Gayet, *Stèles de la XIIe dyn.*, pl. 56).
Daughter *inkw*

VIII/69 ***s3t-ḥi*** [291/11]
Oxford, QC 1113 (Smither – Dakin, *JEA* 25, 1939, 157-165 [163-5; no 4]).[242]
**snb-sw-m-ʿ.i //// mnʿt.f s3t-ḥi*

VIII/70 ***snt*** [296/21]
(Habachi, *Elephantine* IV, no 87, p. 104)
**rn.s-snb m3ʿ-ḫrw mnʿt.f snt*

VIII/71 *swdnt* [303/4]
Turin 1545 (Maspero, *RT* 3, 1882, p. 123 [12]).
**mr pr ḏʿf //// mnʿt.f mrt.f swdnt*
Mother *s3t-nb-sšnw*

VIII/72 ***sbk-nḫt*** / ***w3ḏt*** [304/15] / [74/29]
Elkab, Tomb 8bis (*LD* Text IV, 52).

VIII/73 ***snii*** [310/19]
Paris, Louvre C 168 (Gayet, *Stèles de la XIIe dyn.*, pl. 56).

VIII/74 ***snʿʿ-ib*** [312/14]
Tübingen 462 (ex Stuttgart 12) (Spiegelberg-Pörtner, *AG* I, Tf. 8/12; ANOC 60.2; Brunner-Traut, *Die Ägyptische Sammlung der Universität Tübingen*, 88-90, Tf. 10).
Son *nb-swmnw*

---

[242] Ward, *Feminine Titles,* 8.

VIII/75 ***snbi*** ?   [313/23]
Elkab, Tomb 8bis (*LD* Text IV, 53).
**///sbk-ms mnꜥt.f ḥst.f snbi* (?)

VIII/76 ***snb.tisi***   [314/25]
Paris, Louvre C 13 (N 167) (Spalinger, *RdÉ* 32, 1980, pl. 8, p. 95).
Daughter   *sꜣt.f rn-snb / inn*

VIII/77 ***snb.tisi***   [314/25]
(Petrie, *Season*, no 120).
Mother   *sbk-ḥtp* (?)
Brother   *ḥry-pr sbk-ddw*

VIII/78 ***šꜣy***   [-]
Ashmolean Museum, Oxford 1922.143 (Petrie, *Courtiers*, pl. 12/7).
Daughter   *mẖ(w)*
Son   *ḥr*

VIII/79 ***ḳs-ḥtp***   [-]
(Petrie, *Season*, no 284).
Mother   *ḥtpi*

VIII/80 ***kii-wrt***   [343/4]
London, BM EA 573 (*HT* II, pl. 6).

VIII/81 ***kmnsi***   [345/12]
Cairo, CG 20018 (Lange - Schäfer, *CGC* I, 17-18).

VIII/82 ***gḥst***   [352/19][243]
Paris, Louvre C 173 (Gayet, *Stèles de la XIIe dyn.*, pl. 29).
**mr pr sꜣ-in-ḥrt ///// mnꜥt.f gḥst*
Mother   *ḥmr///*

VIII/83 ***ti-mꜣꜥt***   [-]
(Grdseloff, *JEA* 35, 1949, 59-62).

---

[243] Schneider, *Ausländer in Ägypten* II, 285.

VIII/84 *ṯt.i* [395/5]
Cairo, CG 20457 (Lange - Schäfer, *CGC* II, 54-56).
**ṯ3w n sš ˁn nsw nḫti/////// mnˁt.f ṯt.i*
Son *isi*

VIII/85 ***dd.i-snb*** [402/6]
Marseille 28 (Maspero, *RT* 13, 1890, 117).

VIII/86 ***ddw-ˁnḫ*** [402/16]
Cairo, CG 20724 (Lange - Schäfer, *CGC* II, 353-355).

VIII/87 ***ddt-mwt*** [403/11]
Marseille 28 (Maspero, *RT* 13, 1890, 117).

VIII/88 ***ddt-nb*** [403/14][244]
1) Aswan 1314 (Habachi, *Elephantine* IV, no 84, p. 102).
2) (Petrie, *Courtiers*, pl. 28).
Mother *s3t-sbk*

VIII/89 ***ˁf3*** [416/26]
Wien, KHM ÄS 144 (Hein – Satzinger, *Stelen des Mittleren Reiches I,* 75-80).

VIII/90 ///***mri***
Museum of the Faculty of Letters, Kyoto University, Inv. Nr. 36 (Franke, *MDAIK* 57, 2001, 31-32, Tf. 8a).
Mother *ḥr-m-ḥb*

VIII/91 ///
El Bersheh, Tomb 1(Griffith - Newberry, *El Bersheh* I, pl. 30).

VIII/92 ///
Oldenburg 4403 (Franke, *SAK* 10, 1987, 157-178).

---

[244] Franke, *Heqaib*, 63.

VIII/93 ///
(Petrie, *Season*, no 99).

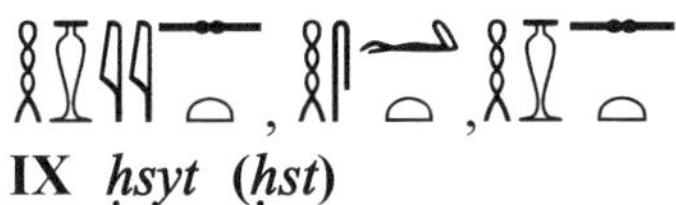

IX ***ḥsyt*** **(*ḥst*)**

Music played a large part in temple and funerary ritual in Ancient Egypt, as well as in everyday entertainment. Both men and women served as musicians, singers or instrumentalists, with evidence dating from the Predynastic period through the Graeco-Roman era.[245] As E. Teeter notes, women who held titles indicating their association with ritual music are very common throughout the dynastic period, attesting to the important role that music played in all manifestations of religion.[246] Furthermore, priestly positions, including temple singers, were one of the few titled offices available to both elite and non-elite women at any period in Egyptian history.[247]

From the Old Kingdom female musicians made up a musical group – *ḫnr*, which functioned in religious as well as in secular context.[248] By the Middle Kingdom, male singers and musicians were also included.

The occurrence of the word *ḥsy* in conjunction with scenes depicting harpists and accompanying singers are known from the Old Kingdom onward.[249] The earliest known evidence of temple singers is found on reliefs in tombs of the Old Kingdom. In that period most of female singers bore the title *ḥsyt*.[250] During the Middle Kingdom, women continued to act as processional musicians, singers (*ḥsyt* and *šmʿyt* though the *šmʿyt* is better documented),[251] various

---

[245] See Manniche, *Music and Musicians*; Emerit, *BIFAO* 102, 2002, 189-210; Robins, *Women in Ancient Egypt*, 120; Teeter, in: *Rediscovering the Muses*, 68-69.

[246] Teeter, in: *The Life of Meresamun*, 29.

[247] Cf. Lorenz, in: *The Life of Meresamun*, 93.

[248] Nord, in: *Studies in Ancient Egypt, the Aegean, and the Sudan*, 137-145; Teeter, in: *Rediscovering the Muses,* 75-76: Robins, *Women in Ancient Egypt*, 148-149 and Fischer, *Egyptian Women*.

[249] Manniche, *Music and Musicians*, figs. 11, 13, 30, 48, 73, pl. 3.

[250] Teeter, in: *The Life of Meresamun*, 25.

[251] See Onstine, *The Role of the Chantress (Smyt)*.

instrumentalists, etc., who performed in the cult.[252] The difference in musical duties of *ḥsyt* and *šmʿyt* is unclear. Groups of singers and harpists are well attested in tomb decoration of the Middle Kingdom.[253] For example, in tomb C1 at Meir four kneeling female musicians are shown in front of Ukhhotep IV and in tomb Qubbet el-Hawa 36 two kneeling women are shown singing.[254]

The holders of the title *ḥsyt* (i.e. *ḥsyt, ḥsyt m dt* and *ḥsyt m bnt*) were probably mainly responsible for entertainment, not for performing music at religious ceremonies.[255] The word *ḥsy* is usually used to describe music making in various contexts, especially scenes that involve harpists who sing to their own music, and scenes where singers accompany a harpist or a mixed ensemble. Furthermore, the term *ḥsy* is also used to describe the singers who accompany flutists and clarinetists.[256] Based on numerous examples it is clear that the *ḥsy* was a designation for an activity that occurred in conjunction with musical performance involving a variety of instruments. The groups of such musicians (including also harpists and clapping women) are recorded on the P. Boulaq 18 (the musical group of the Theban palace of the king)[257] and on two stelae: Paris, Louvre C17 and Ny Calsberg AEIN 964.

Middle Kingdom title-holders were of modest backgrounds and were quite rare. However, the main person on the stela Cairo CG 20257, which belongs to the group of feminine stelae of the Middle Kingdom and Second Intermediate Period,[258] was the singer (*ḥsyt*)

---

[252] Ward, *Index MK*, 1095 (1094, 1096); Id. *Feminine Titles*, 12; Millard, *Position of Women in the Family and in Society,* 289; Quirke, *Titles and bureaux*, 41; Ward, in: *Women's Earliest Records*, 35; Robins, *Women in Ancient Egypt*, 148-149; Markoe - Capel, *Mistress of the House, Mistress of Heaven*. See also Fantechi - Zingarelli, *GM* 186, 2002, 27-35.

[253] Cf. Lichtheim, *JNES* 4, 1945, 178-212; Vasiljević, *SAK* 24, 1997, 313-326; Krah, *Die Harfe im pharaonischen Ägypten*; Assmann, in: *LÄ* II, 972-978; Franke, *Heqaib*, 17. n. 45.

[254] Blackman, *Meir VI*, 21, pl. 19; Parkinson – Franke, in: *Essays in Honor of David B. O'Connor*, 219-235.

[255] Quirke, *The Administration of Egypt*, 95.

[256] Manniche, *Music and Musicians*, figs. 15, 17, 19.

[257] Scharff, *ZÄS* 57, Tf. 5/11.

[258] Stefanović, *GM* 218, 2008, 86-90 and *GM* 220, 2009, 95-98.

s3t-ḥtḥr. Besides the *ḥsyt s3t-ḥtḥr*,[259] several more Middle Kingdom attestations of the title in question are known:

IX/1 ***i.s-ib-nbw*** [12/11]
Marseilles 28 (Maspero, *RT* 13, 1890, 117).

IX/2 ***it*** [48/29]
Paris, Louvre C17 (ANOC 52.2).
**ḥst m dt*[260]

IX/3 ***it*** [48/29]
Paris, Louvre C5 (ANOC 1.7).
**ḥst m bnt*[261]
Mother *ip-nḫnt*

IX/4 ***ʿnḫ.s-n.i*** [67/22]
Paris, Louvre C17 (ANOC 52.2).
**ḥst m dt*

IX/5 ***mrryt*** [162/25]
Paris, Louvre C17 (ANOC 52.2).
**ḥst m dt*

IX/6 ***ḥnwt*** [242/18]
Leiden 30 (V 103) (Boeser, *Leiden* II, Taf. XIII).

IX/7 ***ḫwyt*** [267/16]
TT 60 (Davies, *Antefoker*, pls. 29, 27)
Mother *mkt*

IX/8 ***s3t-imn*** [286/6]
Vatican 22770 [MG 170] (ANOC 65.2).

---

[259] Cf. IX/10.

[260] Ward, *Index MK*, 1094; Fischer, *Egyptian Titles of the Middle Kingdom*, 72.

[261] Ward, *Index MK*, 1096; Id. *Feminine Titles*, 12.

IX/9 ***s3t-imn*** [286/6]
Paris, Louvre C 302 (Ledrain, *Les Monuments Égyptiens*, no 20, pl. VII).

IX/10 ***s3t-ḥtḥr*** [291/14]
Cairo, CG 20257 (Lange - Schäfer, *CCG* I, 276-277).

Son	*s3-imn*
Daughters	*nfr-ḥtp-ʿnkt*
	nbt-tp-iḥw

IX/11 ***sp-n-wrd*** [296/3]
Paris, Louvre C17 (ANOC 52.2).
**ḥst m bnt*

IX/12 ***snbi*** [313/23]
Ny Carlsberg, AEIN 964 (Koefoed-Petersen, *Stele eg. Copenhague*, 16).

IX/13 ***snbt*** [313/27]
Ny Carlsberg, AEIN 964 (Koefoed-Petersen, *Les Stèles égyptiennes*, 16).

IX/14 ***km-ʿšt*** [-]
London, BM EA 67085 (Martin, *Seals*, 1693).

IX/15 ***dw3t-///***
Ny Carlsberg, AEIN 964 (Koefoed-Petersen, *Les Stèles égyptiennes*, 16).

IX/16 ///
London, UC 32120I (vso.) (Collier – Quirke, *The UCL Lahun Papyri: Accounts*, 292-293).

IX/17 ///
London, UC 32146B (Collier – Quirke, *The UCL Lahun Papyri: Accounts*, 254-255).
* *///* *ḥsyt n sḫm-snwsrt-m3ʿ-ḫrw*

IX/18 ///
London, UC 32168 (Collier – Quirke, *The UCL Lahun Papyri: Accounts*, 58-59).

X *ẖtt-pr*

The use of the title *ẖtt-pr* ('cleaning-woman')[262] was limited to the Early Middle Kingdom. By the reign of Senwosret III the *ẖtt-pr* disappeared as a designation of female servants. When being in use along with other female-servant titles, the title *ẖtt-pr* was a mark of a separate class of servants. Due to the fact that the designation *ẖtt-pr* is attested in two Beni Hasan tombs, but not in the Theban tomb of Senet, the wife of Intefiker, O. D. Berlev suggested that the title in question was a local feature. However, he noted that further attestations of the title *ẖtt-pr* do not confirm this opinion.[263]

For Millard it is possible that the provincial nobility may have had some sort of domestic shrines, and the *ẖtt-pr* servant *was attached to such a shrine in some capacity.*[264]

Berlev pointed out that the *ẖtt-pr* domestic servants had free access to every part of the household, i.e. they were servants, which could be deployed anywhere in the household.[265] Thus, it seems that a *ẖtt-pr*, as well as an *ʿḳyt*, had free access to the *šnʿ*. Representations of *ẖtwt-pr* (holders of this title usually appear among offering-beares) make clear that they were responsible for taking the prepared food from the *šnʿ* and bringing it into the dining space of a private house or palace. However, they were not only responsible for the food but also for the dress of their masters.

According to Berlev, the *ẖtt-pr* servants were *meryt*-people, i.e. they were *ḥmwt*. He also draws attention to the fact that many of them bore the names of their masters. As in case of other non-elite

---

[262] Ward, *Index MK*, 1183 (1184); Millard, *Position of Women in the Family and in Society,* 318-319. Cf. also the collective *ẖtwt-pr* as discussed by Gardiner - Sethe, *Letters to the Dead*, 15-16.

[263] Берлев, *Общественные отношения,* 301.

[264] Millard, *Position of Women in the Family and in Society,* 319.

[265] Берлев, *Общественные отношения,* 302; Ward, *Feminine Titles*, 13.

women,[266] the life of the *ẖtt-pr* can be documented through the iconographic and written sources left by those who may have employed them in their houses or estates.

Most attestations of the title *ẖtt-pr* come from the tombs of the Beni Hasan nomarchs, i.e. from the tomb no 2 and no 3. Among the title-holders from the tomb no 3 there is one servant with an extended version of the title: "domestic servant of the chamber of incoming goods".[267] As S. Quirke notes, the Beni Hasan tomb no 3 includes a record of year 6 of Senwosret II – this is the highest dated source for the title *ẖtt-pr*.[268] No data about their family members are recorded.

X/1 ***ỉmỉ*** [25/17]
Beni Hasan, Tomb 2 (Newberry, *Beni Hasan* I, pl. 19).

X/2 ***ỉky*** [48/6]
Beni Hasan, Tomb 2 (Newberry, *Beni Hasan* I, pl. 18).

X/3 ***ỉkw*** [48/9]
Beni Hasan, Tomb 2 (Newberry, *Beni Hasan* I, pl. 18).

X/4 ***ỉt*** [49/3]
Beni Hasan, Tomb 2 (Newberry, *Beni Hasan* I, pl. 19).

X/5 ***ʿnẖ.s*** [67/13]
Paris, Louvre C196 (Gayet, *Stèles de la XIIe dyn.*, pl. 59).

X/6 ***bwt*** [95/3]
Cairo, CG 20024 (Lange-Schäfer, *CGC* I, 26-29).

---

[266] Cf. Teeter, in: *The Life of Meresamun*, 55.

[267] See: Берлев, *Общественные отношения,* 302; Fischer, *Egyptian Studies* I, 76. Compare with Ward's 'scullery-maid of the kitchen' (*Feminine Titles*, 13 and *CdÉ* 57, 1982, 191-200), Millard, *Position of Women in the Family and in Society,* 319, and Quirke, *Titles and bureaux*, 73.

[268] Quire, *Titles and bureaux*, 73.

X/7 ***mrỉ*** [159/21]
Beni Hasan, Tomb 2 (Newberry, *Beni Hasan* I, pl. 20)

X/8 ***ḥrw-nḫt*** [249/10]
Beni Hasan, Tomb 2 (Newberry, *Beni Hasan* I, pl. 18).

X/9 ***ḥtp-ḥḳt*** [259/4]
Beni Hasan, Tomb 2 (Newberry, *Beni Hasan* I, pl. 20).

X/10 ***s3t-ỉmn*** [286/6]
Paris, Louvre C 167 (ANOC 4.5).

X/11***s3t-nb-ỉwnu*** [290/2]
Paris, Louvre C 167 (ANOC 4.5).

X/13 ***sntwtt*** [312/8]
Turin 1626 (1534) (Maspero, *RT* 3, 1882, 115-117, no 107).
Daughter ?

X/12 ***snb-ỉt*** [312/21]
Cairo, CG 23056 (JdE 39589) (Kamal, *Tables d'offrandes*, 49-50).

X/13 ***ṯnt*** [392/8]
Beni Hasan, Tomb 3 (Newberry, *Beni Hasan* I, pl. 35).

X/14 *////*[269]
Beni Hasan, Tomb 3 (Newberry, *Beni Hasan* I, pl. 35).

X/15 *////*[270]
Beni Hasan, Tomb 3 (Newberry, *Beni Hasan* I, pl. 35).

---

[269] Without name.
[270] Ward, *Index MK*, 1184.

XI *ẖkrt-nswt*

The *ẖkrt-nswt* is a feminine designation that becomes very frequent at the end of the Old Kingdom, was commonly in use during the First Intermediate Period, continued through the Middle Kingdom and into the New Kingdom. The title *ẖkrt-nswt* is common on the monuments of the Middle Kingdom and Second Intermediate Period and discussed by several authors.[271] Literally translated as "Royal Ornament", the numerous women thus designated were thought of as concubines belonging to a king's harem. It is now usually accepted that the *ẖkrt-nswt* was rather a *Lady-in-Waiting* initially in the service of a queen.[272]

During the Old and Early Middle Kingdom, they were married women of the upper classes whose husbands were usually part of the king's household or belonged to the upper levels of government.

W. Grajetzki points out that — according to the sources of the Late Middle Kingdom — the title *ẖkrt-nswt* was initially given to women who were closely linked to the royal court, perhaps through some

---

[271] Henry G. Fischer argues that the title means "ornament of the king". He advocates that in several instances *ẖkrwt* are sequestered women who entertained the king by their grace as well as their beauty. However, he points out that it seems unlikely that many of the provincial women who called themselves "sole ornament of the king" had actually been at the court, particularly during the Heracleopolitan Period (Fischer, *Egyptian Women*, 31). For the title and its meaning see: *Wb* III 401/6; Ward, *Index MK*, 1233; Millard, *Position of Women in the Family and in Society,* 274-279; Troy, *Patterns of Queenship*, 77-78, 118; Drenkhahn, *SAK* 4, 1976, 59-67; Nord, *Serapis* 2, 1970, 1-16. *Cf.* Reisner, *Harim*, 17, 88, 118; Brack, *SAK* 11, 1984, 183-186; Ward, *Feminine Titles*, 33-35; Ward, *Berytos* 31, 1983, 74; Vernus, *RdÉ* 26, 1974, 113; Grajetzki, *Two Treasurers*, 49-50; Franke, *JEA* 76, 1990, 229; Fekri, in: *Studies in honor of Ali Radwan.* Vol. 1, 353-374; Willems, *Dayr al-Barsha Volume I*, 72-73; Stefanović, *SAK* 38, 2009; Id. in: *Proceedings of the Tenth International Congress of Egyptologists*.

[272] Drenkhahn, *SAK* 4, 1976, 59-67.

kind of family relationship. After the time of Sebekhotep IV, the title became more popular and perhaps, in some extant, it replaced the title *nbt-pr*.[273] He points out that from the middle of the XIII Dynasty most of the *ẖkrwt-nswt* are no longer directly connected with the royal court and their husbands, in most cases, occupy positions just under the highest officials.[274] The title is also attested in the provinces where it is sometimes found worn by the wives of local dignitaries.[275]

H. Willems suggests that the title could refer to the adorners of the king. *This would not necessarily mean that they belonged to the royal harim, if that existed at all, but perhaps rather that they assisted when the king was being dressed.*[276] According to Willems *it is convincible that such honorific tasks were carried out on a rotational basis by numbers of women belonging to the elite families of the country. This could well explain why so many ẖkr.wt nsw.t are known.*[277] Further more, Willems points out that he is not convinced that the title *ẖkrt-nswt* ever acquired a non-specific connotation like *nbt-pr* or *that the very frequent references in the First Intermediate Period and Early Middle Kingdom to ladies entitled ẖkr.wt nsw.t justify the view that all were true members of the royal family.*[278]

M.M. Fekri, based on the 234 examples of the title in question (25 of them from the Middle Kingdom), comes to the conclusion that the *ẖkrwt-nswt* were of royal origin and that the title should be translated as 'protectrice royal'.[279]

When analysing officials listed with the royal family, as they have been recorded on five lists of P. Boulaq 18 (S1, 11, 18, 38 and 72),[280] St. Quirke observes that the exclusion of families of officials from S1 and S11 indicate a measure of distance from the royal family.[281] The

---

[273] Grajetzki, *Two Treasurers*, 49.

[274] Grajetzki, *Two Treasurers*, 49.

[275] See, for example, stelae Cairo, CG 20539 and New York, MMA 35.7.55

[276] Willems, *Dayr al-Barsha I*, 73.

[277] Willems, *Dayr al-Barsha I*, 73.

[278] Willems, *Dayr al-Barsha I*, 73, n. 49.

[279] Fekri, in: *Studies in Honor of Ali Radwan* I, 353-354, 374.

[280] Quirke, *Administration*, 87-97.

[281] Quirke, *Administration*, 90.

women recorded in this sector do not hold titles such as *nbt-pr* or *ẖkrt nswt*; the list mentions just their names or reference to their husbands. Quirke suggests that *their status or regular designation was implicate in their appearance in their list. For example, the term ẖkr nswt may have denoted a lady of this sector of the palace* (i.e. Inner Palace).[282]

Quirke points out that *it is reasonable to apply the theory that all these families are the relations of functionaries based in the inner Palace.*[283] On the other hand it is also possible that these officials have been attached to the Inner Palace as they and their families resided or ate there.[284] Still, the titles of officials (notable *r nḫn* and *smsw h3yt*) imply the attachment to the palace sector. Quirke also mentions that the attribution of the families in question to the Inner Palace can be explained by the assumption *that the officials attached to that sector would reside in the vicinity, whereas Outer Palace would not.*[285]

Among the cases, which provide possible title-holders to whom to relate families from the papyrus lists, the family of *titi* is perhaps of special importance.[286] The family of *titi* is among those for whom Quirke believes that they belong to the Inner Palace, i.e. to its innermost group.[287] In the lists of P. Boulaq 18, *titi* is recorded as *r nḫn* and *ḫtmty-bity*.[288] The same official is attested on two other monuments with titles *s3b* (*r*) *nḫn*[289] and *s3b*.[290] His wife *iti-ʿnḫ*[291] is recorded in the lists of P. Boulaq 18 without any titles. However, on two other monuments she is termed as *nbt-pr*[292] and *ẖkrt-nswt.*[293] The

[282] Quirke, *Administration*, 90.
[283] Quirkc, *Administration*, 92.
[284] Quirke, *Administration*, 92.
[285] Quirke, *Administration*, 92.
[286] See: Quirke, *Administration*, 91-92; Franke, *Doss.,* 730.
[287] Quirke, *Administration*, 92.
[288] Quirke, *Administration*, 92; Scharff, *ZÄS* 57, 1922, pl. 17**, 15; 27**, 9; 37**, 6; 45**, 4. Cf. Franke, *Doss.,*730.
[289] Peet, *Cem. Abydos* II, 114, fig. 70, pl. 14/4+5.
[290] Peet, *Cem. Abydos* II, 114, fig. 71, pl. 21/10.
[291] See: XI/21.
[292] Peet, *Cem. Abydos* II, 114, fig. 70, pl. 14/4+5.
[293] Peet, *Cem. Abydos* II, 114, fig. 71, pl. 21/10.

absence of title of *ỉtỉ*'s wife in the P. Boulaq 18 speaks in favour of Quirke's idea that her status of *ẖkrt-nswt* was implicate in her appearance in the lists.

The titles of *ỉtỉ-ꜥnḫ*'s husband are very indicative. Based on the list of attestations, four titles are the most frequent among the male members of the *ẖkrwt-nswt* families: *ꜣṯw n ṯt ḥḳꜣ, wr mḏw šmꜥ*, *sꜣb r nḫn* and *sꜣb.*[294]

I Male members of the families of the *ẖkrt-nswt*:

Title	Husband	Father	Son	Brother	
mr ṯbww					> 5
sꜣb					**< 10**
ꜣṯw n ṯt ḥḳꜣ					**< 25**
sꜣ-nswt					< 5
sš ḥnw-nṯr					> 5
wr mḏw šmꜥ					**<25**
sꜣb r nḫn					**<10**
mr šnt n ḥwt-nṯr					> 5
ꜣṯw ꜥꜣ n nỉwt					> 5
sḥḏ šmsw					> 5
wꜥb n ỉmn					> 5
ỉry-pꜥt ḥꜣty-ꜥ sꜣb sḥḏ sš					> 10
ḥry-sštꜣ r nḫn					> 5
rḫ-nswt mꜣꜥ					> 5
mr ṯbww					> 5
ḥm-nṯr n ḥr-bhdt					> 5
ḥrỉ-ḥb					> 5
sš					> 5
ḥm-nṯr					> 5
mr ḫnww					> 5
wꜥb					> 5
mr nbw					> 5

[294] See: Ward, *Feminine Titles*, 37; Vernus, *RdÉ* 26, 1974, 113; Grajetzki, *Two Treasurers*, 49.

sḥd ḥm-nṯr tpy n ḥr nḫn mr ꜣhwt					> 5
sš wr n mr ḫtmt					> 5
sš ḏꜥtt sš ḥwt-nṯr					> 5
ḥꜣty-ꜥ ḫtmty-bỉty smr wꜥty mr mšꜥ					> 5

These titles, which are very common for the husbands, fathers, sons and brothers of the *ḫkrwt-nswt*[295], seem to belong to the highest social level during the late Middle Kingdom and Second Intermediate Period, and perhaps demonstrate the approach to the court circles or royal household. The majority of these men held the title *ꜣṯw n ṯt ḥḳꜣ* (for a family tree see plate 3). This 'title pairing', already recognised by W. Ward, in husband-wife relationship,[296] was current especially in the late Middle Kingdom and Second Intermediate Period[297].However, it is also important to note that two of the aforementioned titles (i.e. *ꜣṯw n ṯt ḥḳꜣ* and *wr mḏw šmꜥ*) are the most common late Middle Kingdom / Second Intermediate Period titles attested for men. Based on this fact, it can be concluded that the 'recognised title pairing' is the effect of the level of attestations of the titles. On the other hand, nearly 70% of the female title-holders recorded on the monuments of *ꜣṯw n ṯt ḥḳꜣ* bear the title *ḫkrt-nswt*. With *wr mḏw šmꜥ*, the title *nbt-pr* is predominant.[298]

---

[295] Vernus, *RdÉ* 26, 1974, 113; cf. Quirke, *Administration*, 99, n. 8.

[296] Ward, *Feminine Titles*, 37. W. Helck notes that in the XVIII Dynasty the *ḫkrt-nswt* were generally chosen from unimportant families hence were brought into the harem for their beauty rather than family connections. They were then married off to high officials to bind the latter more closely to the Palace (Helck, *Militärführer in der 18. ägyptischen Dynastie*, 70). W. Ward points out that this does not apply to earlier periods (Ward, *Berytos* 31, 1983, 73, n. 44). Cf. Petrie, *Abydos I*, 42; Ward, *Feminine Titles*, 22, 25, 37; Vernus, *RdÉ* 26, 1974, 113; Grajetzki, *Two Treasurers*, 49.

[297] Chiddingston EDECC:01.2882; *cf.* Grajetzki, in: *IBAES* V, 62-65.

[298] Stefanović, in: *Proceedings of the Tenth International Congress of Egyptologists* (forthcoming).

II Female members of the families of the *ꜣṯw n ṯt ḥḳꜣ*

Title	Mother	Wife	Daughter	Sister	
ꜥnḫt nt nswt tpt					= 1
wbꜣyt n ḥr					= 1
nbt pr					= < 8
ỉryt-pꜥt					= 3
ẖkrt-nswt					**= <30**
sꜣt ḥꜣty-ꜥ					=1
sꜣt-nswt					=1

The title *ꜣṯw n ṯt ḥḳꜣ* belongs to the group of regular military titles of the Middle Kingdom and the Second Intermediate Period. In his article, *The Navy of the Middle Kingdom* (in Russian), O. D. Berlev demonstrated that the title in question involved the commanders of the royal navy forces on the river, and not a 'recipient' or 'controller' of the ruler's table.[299] Berlev pointed out that Egyptian military organisation of the Middle Kingdom was of amphibious nature and that its foundation was the fleet. Warfare was oriented to the Nile and the king's flotilla, with the *ꜣṯw n ṯt ḥḳꜣ*, played the key role in transport. Thus, the engagement in the royal navy was attractive to the members of the high-ranking and royal families and some of them, especially during the late Middle Kingdom and Second Intermediate Period, held the title *ꜣṯw n ṯt ḥḳꜣ*.[300]

St. Quirke, analysing the same title, considers the *ꜣṯw n ṯt ḥḳꜣ* as the *commander of the crew of the ruler*, i.e. the officer of the national forces. This interpretation would account directly for the higher standing of the *ꜣṯw n ṯt ḥḳꜣ* within the hierarchy of military commanders of the late Middle Kingdom and Second Intermediate Period, as it is attested, for example, in accounts of P. Boulaq 18.[301]

299 Берлев, *ПС* 17, 1976, 6-19.

300 Берлев, *ПС* 17, 1976, 6-20; Berlev, *RdÉ* 23, 1971, 23-48.

301 Quirke, *The Administration of Egypt*, 82.

The *ꜣṯw n ṯt ḥḳꜣ* would, according to Quirke, form the second tier of military command, below the *mr mšꜥ* and above the *ꜣṯw n nỉwt.*[302]

However, it is important to note that rank titles are not so often attested, according to their dossiers, within the titularies of the Middle Kingdom and Second Intermediate Period *commanders of the crew of the ruler*. The titles of the members of the families of the *ꜣṯw n ṯt ḥḳꜣ*, both female and male (many of them bearing the same title), refer to various sectors of the administration.[303]

III The *ḫkrt-nswt* on the monuments of the *ꜣṯw n ṯt ḥḳꜣ*[304]

Records	Mother	Wife	Sister	Daughter	Relative
Berlin 7287 & Vienna KHM ÄS 196					
Bristol H 521					
Brussels E 480					
CCG 20322					
CCG 20530					
CCG 20668 & Petrie, *Abydos I*, 42, pl. LIX					
CCG 28030					
Chicago, Field Museum 31.679					
Chicago, OIM 6740					
Chiddingston Castle, EDECC:01.2882					

[302] Quirke, *Titles and bureaux*, 97

[303] As for the prosopography of the holders of this title as contained in the works of Chevereau, *RdÉ* 43, 1992, 23-30, nos. 411-480, Stefanović, *Military Titles*, nos. 398-480 and Id., in: *Proceedings of the Xth International Congress of Egyptologists*, there can be added five more person: Ball, *Light From the East*, 76-77 (Newberry, *PSBA* 25, 1903, 135-136); Cornell University Anthropology Collections REX030/193 (unpublished); Elkab Tomb, 8 bis (*LD* Text V, 52-54); lower part of stela Leeds, City Museum (*PM* VIII/3, no. 803-029-800 – two attestations).

[304] Cf. Chevereau, *RdÉ* 43, 1992, n° 470, 431, 427, 417, 480, 460, 454, 425, 435, 418, 452, 462, 467; D. Franke, *Doss.*, 718, 312a, 576, 223(b-c), 224, 578; Stefanović, *Military Titles*, 471, 426, 419, 406, 480, 462, 452, 417, 447, 428, 408, 449, 423, 460, 436, 454, 464, 465.

Engelbach, *ASAE* 23, 1923, 183-186					
Esna 224E					
Krakow MNK XI-490 (a)					
Krakow MNK XI-490 (b)					
Liverpool M 14001					
Moscow 5608					
Elkab, Tomb 8bis					

Unfortunately, it is true that our understanding of the issue of the social position of the *ẖkrt-nswt*, as well as of many other non-royal feminine titls, is still very limited. The majority of the known female titles do not appear in any explanatory context and cannot be understood with accuracy. Since the meaning and function of women's titles are often unknown, the duties and the rank of an individual can rarely be determined. On the other hand, from the methodological point of view, it is very important to make a clear dinstinction between *ẖkrt-nswt, ẖkrt-nswt wꜥtt* and the title sequence *ẖkrt-nswt* (*wꜥtt*) *ḥmt-nṯr ḥtḥr*. These designations do not refer to one and the same 'position' or 'rank', as they are treated in the Fekri's study,[305] and must be analised within their chronological framework. The *ẖkrt-nswt* of the First Intermediate Period and the *ẖkrt-nswt* of the Late Middle Kingdom are not the same in respect to the social context they belonged, the level of attestations, the types of monuments etc. The changes in the social status (royal vs. non-royal usage) and number of women who bore the title indicate that the Egyptians perceived the role and status of the title *ẖkrt-nswt* differently through time.

It is also important to note that there are a number of cases where the women held the title *ẖkrt-nswt* for several generations. This perhaps demonstrates that the title was not held by a single person in the family but rather transferred in a single line of inheritance. For

[305] Fekri, in: *Studies in Honor of Ali Radwan* I, 353-374. See also Millard, *Position of Women in the Family and in Society,* 274-279.

instance, if the mother was *ẖkrt-nswt*, at least one daughter was *ẖkrt-nswt* as well.

IV Female members of the families of the *ẖkrt-nswt*:

	Mother	Daughter	Sister	Daughter-in-Law
ẖkrt-nswt				
ꜥnḫt nt nswt tpt				
bꜣkt nt ḥḳꜣ				
sꜣt-nswt				
wbꜣyt ḥr				
ỉryt-pꜥt				

In the list of attestations that follows, 106 *ẖkrwt-nswt* are recorded.[306]

XI/1 *ỉꜣm-rs* [-]
Elkab, Tomb 8bis (*LD* Text IV, 54).
Husband *ꜣṯw n ṯt ḥḳꜣ bbỉ*

XI/2 *ỉꜥ-ỉb* [11/19]
Cairo, CG 20322 (Lange-Schäfer, *CGC* I, 334-335).
Husband *mr ṯbww rn.f-rs*

XI/3 *ỉꜥ-ỉb* [11/19]
Cairo, JdE 33507 & Cairo, JdE 33509 (Northampton, *Theban Necropolis*, pl. XVI).

XI/4 *ỉꜥt-ỉb* [11/23]
Esna 215E (Downes, *Excavations Esna*, 73, fig. 37).
Husband *sꜣb*

306 Compare with Ward, *Feminine Titles*, 33-35, Vernus, *RdÉ* 26, 1974, 113 and Stefanović, *SAK* 38, 2009.

XI/5 ***iꜥt-ib*** [11/23]
Berlin, Äegyptisches Museum 32/66 (Kaiser, *Äegyptisches Museum Berlin*, 42 [426]).

Husband	*ḫtmty-bity mr gs-pr rn-snb*
Son	*ḫtmty-bity mr gs-pr mnṯw-ḥtp*

XI/6 ***iꜥt-ib*** [11/23]
London, UC 14214 (Petrie, *Qurneh*, pl. XXX/6).

XI/7 ***iw-snb*** [13/27]
Chicago, Field Museum 31679 (Allen, *Field Museum Stelae*, 20-23, pl. 7/13).

Husband	*ꜣṯw n ṯt ḥḳꜣ sbk*
Sons	*sꜣb nmw*
	sꜣb ///
	sꜣb ḫnmw-ms
	sꜣb ḫnmw
	sꜣb ///bb-snb
	sꜣm mry-ḫmnw
	sꜣb ḥr

XI/8 ***iw-snb*** [15/22]
Paris, Louvre C13 (N 167) (Spalinger, *RdÉ* 32, 1980, 95 pl. 8; Bennett, *GM* 151, 1996, 19-22).

XI/9 ***iw-ddi*** [-]
Durham N 1984 (Bourriau, *Pharaohs and Mortals*, 66).

Son	*sꜣ-nswt bb*

XI/10 ***iwy-rs*** [16/17]
(Peet, *Cem. Abydos* II, 115-116, pl. 24, fig. 73*).

XI/11 ***iwḥt-ib*** [18/17]
London, BM EA 1163 (*HT* IV, 18-21).

Husband	*sš ḥnw-nṯr sbk-ḥtp*

XI/12 ***iwḥt-ib*** [18/17]
Cairo, CG 20661 (Lange-Schäfer, *CGC* II, 292-293).

Husband wr mḏw šmꜥ ib(.i)-iꜥ(.w)
Son ? s3b r nḫn rs-nfr

XI/13 *ib(.i)-iꜥ(.w)* [19/4]
Cairo, JdE 37507 (Legrain, *RT* 24, 1902, 213).

Mother	*ẖkrt-nswt sbk-rs*
Father ?	*ḫtmty nṯr n imn snb.f*
Brothers ?	*sš ḫtmt nṯr ḏhwti*
	r nḫn snb-ḥnꜥ.f
	r nḫn imn-m-s3w
Sisters ?	*ẖkrt-nswt nḥti*
	ẖkrt-nswt ḫnsw

XI/14 *ibr*////
Cairo, CG 20486 (Lange-Schäfer, *CGC* II, 81-82).

XI/15 *ipi* [23/13]
(Budge, *Egyptian Antiquities in the possession of Lady Meux*, no 185, 96-98).

Husband	*mr šnt n ḥwt-nṯr ddi-rs*
Son	*s3b r nḫn ddi-rs*
Daughter-in-law	*ẖkrt-nswt nbw-m-ḫꜥi.s*

XI/16 *in-it.f* [34/1]
(Jacquet-Gordon, *Karnak-Nord* VIII, no 110, p. 171-175*).

Father ?	*s3-nswt imn-ḥ3t*

XI/17 *in-it.f* [34/1]
Würzburg N.35 (Берлев, *ПС* 25, 1974, 26-31).

XI/18 *ir-tm-ib* [-]
Paris, Louvre AF 9916 (Delange, *Cat. statues ég. M. E.*, 220-223).

Husband	*sš ḥwt-nṯr ẖnmw-m-ḥ3t*
Son	*sš ḥwt-nṯr ẖnmw-ḥtp*

XI/19 *iri*///
1) Berlin 7287 (*AIB* I, 203; ANOC 65.4)

2) Wien, KHM ÄS 196 (Hein – Satzinger, *Stelen des Mittleren Reiches* I, 133-138).

Husband	*ꜣṯw n ṯt ḥḳꜣ kms*[307]
Sons	*sꜣb r nḫn bmbw*
	wr mḏw šmꜥ jḳj
	wr mḏw šmꜥ sꜣ///
	[*wr mḏw šmꜥ nb*]-*snt*

XI/20 ***irmhi*** [-]
Chicago, Field Museum 239003 (Martin, *Seals*, 270).

XI/21 ***iti-ꜥnḫ*** [-]
1) (Peet, *Cem. Abydos* II, 114, fig. 71, pl. 21/10).
2) (Peet, *Cem. Abydos* II, 114, fig. 70, pl. 14/4+5).
3) P. Boulaq XVII (Scharff, *ZÄS* 57, 1922, pl. 27**, 2; 17**, 2.19; 44, 2).

* *nbt-pr* (doc. 2)	
Husband	*sꜣb titi*[308]

XI/22 ***ꜥkw*** [71/30]
Cairo, CG 20058 (Lange-Schäfer, *CGC* I, 72-73).

XI/23 ***ꜥkw*** [71/30]
Cairo, CG 20058 (Lange-Schäfer, *CGC* I, 72-73).

Mother	*gti*

XI/24 ***bn-ḥr-inḏ-ib*** [97/1]
Cairo, CG 20486 (Lange-Schäfer, *CGC* II, 81-82).

XI/25 ***ptḥ-ḳni*** [-]
Cairo, CG 20373 (JdE 25450) (Lange-Schäfer, *CGC* I, 374-376; ANOC 77.1).

Husband	*mr šnt n ḥwt-nṯr ddi-rs*[309]
Sons	*mr šnt n ḥwt-nṯr nt inpw sbk-ḥtp*[310]

---

[307] Cf. Franke, *Doss*., 718.
[308] Cf. Franke, *Doss*., 730.
[309] Cf. Franke, *Doss*., 740.

	wr mḏw šmꜥ nn.i
Daughter-in-law	*ẖkrt-nswt nbw-m-ḥ3b*[311]

XI/26 ***mw-nw-ib*** [147/1]
London, UC 11353 (Martin, *Seals*, 540).

XI/27 ***mwt.i-ꜥnḫti*** [148/20]
Moscow 5608 (Hodjash - Berlev, *Pushkin Museum*, no 38).

Husband	*3ṯw n ṯt ḥḳ3 sn-rdiw*
Daughter	*ꜥnḫt nt nswt tpt wḏ-h3w*
Sons	*s3b r nḫn snbi*
	3ṯw ꜥ3 n niwt snb-it.f
	sḥḏ šmsw ib(.i)-iꜥ(w)

XI/28 ***mwt.j-snb.ti*** [149/1]
Berkeley CA, Phoebe Apperson Hearst Museum of Anthropology, 6.19888 (Lutz, *Tomb Steles*, no 80).

Mother	*b3kt nt ḥḳ3 w3ḏt m3ꜥt-ḫrw*

XI/29 ***mntw-ḥtp*** [154/21]
Turin 1626 (1534) (Maspero, *RT* 3, 1882, 115-117, no 107).

XI/30 ***mr.s*** [158/5]
Cairo, CG 28028 (Daressy, *RT* 14, 1893, 35).

XI/31 ***n-ib-nbw*** [170/30]
(Jacquet-Gordon, *Karnak-nord* VIII, 171-175, no 110).

Husband	*wꜥb n imn imn-ꜥ3*
Son ?	*wꜥb n imn nb-iri-r-3w*

XI/32 ***n-ib-nbw*** [170/30]
Bolton 1920.10.12 (ex 10.20.12) (Stefanović, *SAK* 2009)

Husband	*rḫ nswt m3ꜥ rn-snb*

XI/33 ***n-ḳr-ḥri-jb*** [-]

---

[310] Cf. Franke, *Doss.*, 584.
[311] Cf. Franke, *Doss.*, 584.

Liverpool, M 13635 (Grajetzki, *Two Treasurers*, pl. 2, p. 28).

Husband	?
Daughter	*s3t-nswt s3-ḫnt-ḫty*

XI/34 ***nbt-iwnt*** [187/23]

Cairo, CG 20668 (Lange-Schäfer, *CCG* II, 297).

Mother	*ẖkrt-nswt nfrt-wbn.s*
Father	*3ṯw n ṯt ḥḳ3 sbk-ḥtp*
Brother	*s3b r nḫn rʿi*

XI/35 ***nbt-iwnt*** [187/23]

Chicago, OIM 6740 (Garstang, *El-Arabah*, pl. XIII).

Husband	*3ṯw n ṯt ḥḳ3 bbi*

XI/36 ***nbt-m-///***

Chiddingston Castle, EDECC:01.2882 (Grajetzki, in: *IBAES* V, 62-65).

Mother	*ẖkrt-nswt sm-ib*
Father	*iry-pʿt ḥ3ty-ʿ s3b sḥḏ sš s3-imn*
Brothers	*3ṯw n ṯt ḥḳ3 s3-imn / rs*
	wr mḏw šmʿ imny-šry
	wr mḏw šmʿ wḏ-h3w
Sisters	*ẖkrt-nswt ḫnswt*
	ẖkrt-nswt nb-htp.ty
	ẖkrt-nswt nb-mtr
	ẖkrt-nswt sbk-ṯ3w.s

XI/37 ***nbw-ʿ3-ib*** [-]

(Jacquet-Gordon, *Karnak-nord* VIII, 176-179, no 111).

Husband	*ḥry-sšt3 r nḫn dd-nbw*

XI/38 ***nbw-m-wsḫ.t*** [190/23]

Bristol H 521 (Randall-Maciver-Mace, *El Amrah and Abydos*, 86, pl. 38).

Mother	*wb3yt ḥr šnb.tisi*
Father	*3ṯw n ṯt ḥḳ3 rn-snb*

XI/39 ***nbw-m-ḫb*** [191/5]
1) Cairo, CG 20778 (Lange-Schäfer, *CGC* II, 407-408; ANOC 77. 2)
2) (Budge, *Egyptian Antiquities in the possession of Lady Meux*, 96-98, no 185).

Husband	*mr šnt n ḥwt-nṯr nt inpw sbk-ḥtp*[312]

XI/40 ***nbw-m-ḫꜥi.s*** [191/6]
(Budge, *Egyptian Antiquities in the possession of Lady Meux*, 96-98, no 185).

Husband	*sꜣb r nḫn ddi-rs*

XI/41 ***nbw-m-tḫ(.t)*** [191/9]
Chicago, OIM 7779 (Petrie, *Abydos* I, pl. 60/4)

Sisters ?	*ẖkrt-nswt sꜣt-imn*
	ẖkrt-nswt nb-ḫꜥi.s

XI/42 ***nbw-mtr*** [-]
Chiddingston Castle, EDECC:01.2882 (Grajetzki, in: *IBEAS* V, 62-65).

Mother	*ẖkrt-nswt sm-ib*
Father	*iry-pꜥt ḥꜣty-ꜥ sꜣb sḥḏ sš sꜣ-imn*
Brothers	*ꜣṯw n ṯt ḥkꜣ sꜣ-imn / rs*
	wr mḏw šmꜥ imny-šry
	wr mḏw šmꜥ wḏ-hꜣw
Sisters	*ẖkrt-nswt nbt-m-///*
	ẖkrt-nswt ḫnswt
	ẖkrt-nswt nbw-ḥtp.ty
	ẖkrt-nswt sbk-ṯꜣw.s

XI/43 ***nbw-r-mni*** [-]
(Franke, *Heqaib*, 87, Tf. 9).

XI/44 ***nbw-ḥr-mr.s*** ? [-]
Cairo, CG 20486 (Lange-Schäfer, *CGC* II, 81-82).

XI/45 ***nbw-ḥr-rdi*** [191/19]

---

[312] Cf. Franke, *Doss.*, 584.

1) Cairo, CG 28030 (Lacau, *Sarcophages*, 79).
2) Cairo, CG 28109 (Lacau, *Sarcophages*, 87-88).

Husband	*ꜣṯw n ṯt ḥḳꜣ ///*

XI/46 *nbw-ḥr-š.s* [191/23]
(Vandekerckhove – Müller-Wollermann, *Eklab* VI, 32, F16).

Husband	*rḫ nswt sbk-nḫt*

XI/47 *nbw-ḥtp.ti* [192/1]
Cairo, CG 20322 (Lange-Schäfer, *CGC* I, 334-335).

Husband	*sꜣb r nḫn rri-rs*
Son	*mr ṯbww rn.f-rs*

XI/48 *nbw-ḥtp.ti* [192/1]
Cairo, CG 20322 (Lange-Schäfer, *CGC* I, 334-335).

Husband	*mr ṯbww rn.f-rs*

XI/49 *nbw-ḥtp.ti* [192/1]
Chiddingston Castle, EDECC:01.2882 (Grajetzki, in: *IBAES* V, 62-65).

Mother	*ẖkrt-nswt sm-ib*
Father	*iry-pꜥt ḥꜣty-ꜥ sꜣb sḥḏ sš sꜣ-imn*
Brothers	*ꜣṯw n ṯt ḥḳꜣ sꜣ-imn / rs*
	wr mḏw šmꜥ imny-šry
	wr mḏw šmꜥ wḏ-hꜣw
Sisters	*ẖkrt-nswt nbt-m-///*
	ẖkrt-nswt ḫnswt
	ẖkrt-nswt nbw-mtr
	ẖkrt-nswt sbk-ṯꜣw.s

XI/50 *nbw-ḫꜥi.s* [192/3]
Cairo, CG 20322 (Lange-Schäfer, *CGC* I, 334-335).

Husband	*mr ṯbww rn.f-rs*

XI/51 *nbw-ḫꜥi.s* [192/3]
Cairo, CG 20530 (Lange-Schäfer, *CCG* II, 131-135; Trapani, in: *Proceedings of the Ninth International Congress of Egyptologists*, 1827-1838).

Mother | *b3kt nt ḥḳ3 t3-ḥnwt*
Husband | *ḥm-nṯr n ḥr-bhdt ḥr-m-mḥ-ỉb*
Sons | *3ṯw n ṯt ḥḳ3 ///*
3ṯw n ṯt ḥḳ3 ỉw-snb-p///
ḥry-ḥb sn.ỉ
sš sbk-ḥtp
ḥm-nṯr ḥrw-3w-ỉb

XI/53 ***nbw-ḫʿỉ.s*** [192/3]
Chicago, OIM 7779 (Petrie, *Abydos* I, pl. 60/4).
Sisters ? | *ẖkrt-nswt s3t-ỉmn*
ẖkrt-nswt nbw-m-tḫ(.t)

XI/54 ***nbw-ḫʿỉ.s*** [192/3]
Private Collection, Tadross (Vernus, *RdÉ* 26, 1974, 101-114).
Husband | *s3b r nḫn sbk-m-ḥb*

XI/55 ***nbw-ḫʿỉ.s-mw-ỉb*** ?[-]
Cairo, CG 20486 (Lange-Schäfer, *CGC* II, 81-82).

XI/56 ***nbw-k3w-rʿ*** [192/9]
Bonn, Ägyptisches Museum der Universität L 1675 (Lapp, *MDAIK* 50, 1994, 231-252, Tf. 37-41).
Mother | *nbt-pr ḥnwt-pw*
Brother | *mr ḫnww snʿʿ-ỉb*

XI/57 ***nfr-ḥtp*** [198/14]
Cairo, JdE 33480 (Northampton, *Theban Necropolis*, pls. XV, XVI).

XI/58 ***nfr-ḥtp*** [198/14]
Esna 216E (Downes, *Excavations Esna 1905-1906,* 74, fig. 38).
Husband | *s3b ỉtf-rs*

XI/59 ***nfrt*** [201/10]

(Hayes, *The Scepter of Egypt* I, 348).[313]

XI/60 ***nfrt-wbn*** [201/22]
London, UC 14418 (Stewart, *Petrie Collection* II, 27 [113], pl. 28 [3]).

XI/61 ***nfrt-wbn.s*** [201/23][314]
1) Cairo, CG 20668 (Lange-Schäfer, *CCG* II, 297).
2) (Petrie, *Abydos* I, pl. LIX)

Husband	*3ṯw n ṯt ḥḳ3 sbk-ḥtp*
Son	*s3b r nẖn r^ci*
Daughter	*ẖkrt-nswt nbt-iwn.t*

XI/62 ***nfrt-wbn.s*** [201/23]
Elkab, Tomb 8bis (*LD* Text V, 54).

Husband	*s3-nswt ///// mnṯw-nẖt*
Father	*3ṯw n ṯt ḥḳ3 bbi*
Mother ?	*ẖkrt-nswt sbk-nẖt*

XI/63 ***nfrt-wbn.s*** [201/23]
Engelbach, *ASAE* 23, 1923, 183-186.

Husband	*3ṯw n ṯt ḥḳ3 rᶜ-msw*

XI/64 ***nfrt.si-m-ib*** [-]
Esna 224E (Downes, *Excavations Esna*, 76, fig. 40).

Husband ?	*3ṯw n ṯt ḥḳ3 ipw*
Son	*s3-nswt ḥr*
	s3-nswt sbk-m-ḥb
	3ṯw n ṯt ḥḳ3 s3-wnis

XI/65 ***nfrw*** [203/18]
Krakow MNK XI-490 (Luft, *ZÄS* 115, 1988).

Mother	*ẖkrt-nswtt sbk-m-ḥb*

[313] "The royal ornament Nyet-nefret", compare Willems, *Chests of Life*, 33, T5NY.
[314] Franke, *Doss.*, no 576.

XI/66 ***nfrw*** [203/18]
Paris, Louvre C13 (N.167) (Spalinger, *RdÉ* 32, 1980, 95 pl. 8; Bennett, *GM* 151, 1996, 19-22).

XI/67 ***nfrw*** [203/18]
Manchester 4424 (unpublished).

Husband	*ddtw*

XI/68 ***nfrw-sbk*** [204/3]
Cairo, CG 20530 (Lange-Schäfer, *CCG* II, 131-135; Trapani, in: *Proceedings of the Ninth International Congress of Egyptologists*, 1827-1838).

Husband	*ḥm-nṯr snb*
Son	*ḥm-nṯr n ḥr-bhdt ḥr-m-mḥ-ỉb*

XI/69 ***nnỉ*** [205/26]
Brooklyn NY, Brooklyn Museum of Fine Arts, 44.123.96 (Martin, *Seals*, 755).

XI/70 ***nḥsỉ(t)*** [-]
Liebienghaus Museum, Frankfurt IN 2607e (*Liebieghaus Museum. Ägyptische Bildwerke III*, no 28).

Husband	*wꜥb mnṯw-ḥtp*

XI/71 ***nḫtỉ*** ? [209/7]
Cairo, JdE 37507 (Legrain, *RT* 24, 1902, 213).

Mother	*ẖkrt-nswt sbk-rs*
Father ?	*ḫtmty nṯr n ỉmn snb.f*
Brothers ?	*sš ḫtmt nṯr ḏhwtỉ*
	r nḫn snb-ḥnꜥ.f
	r nḫn ỉmn-m-sꜣw
Sisters ?	*ẖkrt-nswt ỉb-ỉꜥw*
	ẖkrt-nswt ḫnsw

XI/72 ***nḫty*** [212/1]
Paris, Louvre AF 9919 (Delange, *Cat. statues ég. M. E.*, 226).

XI/73 ***r-ḥtp-nbw*** [-]

Cairo, JdE 75193 (Martin, *Seals*, 809).

XI/74 ***rn-snb*** [222/26]
London, BM EA 1348 (Bourriau, *Pharaohs and Mortals*, 57-59, no 45).

XI/75 ***ḥ3t-špswt*** [232/23]
Krakow MNK XI-490 (Luft, *ZÄS* 115, 1988).

Husband	*3ṯw n ṯt ḥḳ3 rn.f-snb*
Son	*3ṯw n ṯt ḥḳ3 sbk-m-ḥb*
Daughter	*ẖkrt-nswt sbk-m-ḥb*

XI/76 ***ḥpw*** [238/14]
Athens, National Archaeological Museum, 135 (Pörtner, *Athen und Konstantinopel,* III/10).

Husband	*wr mḏw šmᶜ ddtw-sbk*
Daughter ?	*ẖkrt-nswt sbk-ḥtp*

XI/77 ***ḥpw*** [238/14]
Randall-Maciver - Mace, *El Amrah and Abydos*, pl. 34/2.

Husband	*mr nbw ///*

XI/78 ***ḥnwt*** [242/18]
Cairo, JdE 37507 (Legrain, *RT* 24, 1902, 213).

XI/79 ***ḥr(?)-m-ḥb*** [248/7]
Cairo, CG 20732 (Lange-Schäfer, *CCG* II, 362).

Husband	*s3-nswt tpi nḫt-sbk*

XI/80 ***ḥtp///***
Brussels E 480 (Petrie, *Abydos* II, 44, pl. XXX/5).

XI/81 ***ḥtp-ḥrw*** [250/7]
Brussels E 480 (Petrie, *Abydos* II, 44, pl. XXX/5).

XI/82 ***ḫnsw*** [270/16]
London, UC 14418 (Stewart, *Petrie Collection* II, 27 [113], pl. 28 [3]).

Son s3b r nḫn nḥi

XI/83 *ḫnsw* [270/16]
Cairo, JdE 37507 (Legrain, *RT* 24, 1902, 213).

Mother	*ẖkrt-nswt sbk-rs*
Father ?	*ḫtmty-nṯr n imn snb.f*
Brothers ?	*sš ḫtmt nṯr ḏhwti*
	r nḫn snb-ḥnᶜ.f
	r nhn imn-m-s3w
Sisters ?	*ẖkrt-nswt ib-iᶜw*
	ẖkrt-nswt nḥti ?

XI/84 *ḫnsw* [270/16]
1) Moscow 5358 & Moscow 5359 (Berlev, *JEA* 60, 1974, 106-113 pl. XIII).
2) Cairo, CG 28028 (Lacau, *Sarcophages*, 69-71).

Husband	*rḫ nswt*[315]

XI/85 *ḫnswt* [-]
Chiddingston Castle, EDECC:01.2882 (Grajetzki, in: *IBAES* V, 62-65).

Mother	*ẖkrt-nswt sm-ib*
Father	*iry-pᶜt ḥ3ty-ᶜ s3b sḥḏ sš s3-imn*
Brothers	*3ṯw n ṯt ḥk3 s3-imn / rs*
	wr mḏw šmᶜ imny-šry
	wr mḏw šmᶜ wḏ-h3w
Sisters	*ẖkrt-nswt nbt-m-///*
	ẖkrt-nswt nb-htp.ty
	ẖkrt-nswt nb-mtr
	ẖkrt-nswt sbk-ṯ3w.s
Son ?	*s3-nswt sbk-ḥtp*

XI/86 *s3t-imn* [286/6]
Chicago, OIM 7779 (Petrie, *Abydos* I, pl. 60/4).

Sisters ?	*ẖkrt-nswt nbw-m-tḫ(.t)*
	ẖkrt-nswt nb-ḫᶜi.s

[315] Franke, *Doss.,* 655; Grajetzki, *Zentralverwaltung*, 180 (XI.6).

XI/87 ***sꜣt-wrwt*** [288/1]
(Arnold, *EA* 9, 1996, 23-25).

XI/88 ***sbk-m-ḥb*** [304/5]
Krakow MNK XI-490 (Luft, *ZÄS* 115, 1988, 147-153).

Father	*ꜣṯw n ṯt ḥḳꜣ nb-ỉry-r-ꜣw*
Mother	*ỉryt-pꜥt mnṯw-ḥr-ḫnt*
Brother	*ꜣṯw n ṯt ḥḳꜣ sbk-nḫt*

XI/89 ***sbk-m-ḥb*** [304/5]
Krakow MNK XI-490 (Luft, *ZÄS* 115, 1988, 147-153).

Mother	*ẖkrt-nswt ḥꜣt-špswt*
Father	*ꜣṯw n ṯt ḥḳꜣ rn.f-snb*
Brother	*ꜣṯw n ṯt ḥḳꜣ sbk-m-ḥb*

XI/90 ***sbk-nḫt*** [304/15]
New York, MMA 35.5.55 (Hayes, *JEA* 33, 1947, 4-5).

Husband	*sḥd ḥm-nṯr tpy n ḥr nḫn mr ꜣḥwt* *ḥr-m-ḫꜥ.w.f*

XI/91*sbk-nḫt* [304/15]
Elkab, Tomb 8bis (*LD* Text IV, 52-54).

Husband	*ꜣṯw n ṯt ḥḳꜣ bbỉ*
Daughter ?	*ẖkrt-nswt nfrt-wbn.s*

XI/92 ***sbk-rs*** [305/1]
Cairo, JdE 37507 (Legrain, *RT* 24, 1902, 213).

Husband ?	*ḫtmty nṯr n ỉmn snb.f*
Sons ?	*sš ḫtmt nṯr ḏhwtỉ*
	r nḫn snb-ḥnꜥ.f
	r nhn ỉmn-m-sꜣw
Daughters ?	*ẖkrt-nswt nḥtỉ ?*
	ẖkrt-nswt ḫnsw
	ẖkrt-nswt ỉb-ỉꜥw

XI/93 ***sbk-ḥtp*** [305/6]
Athens, National Archaeological Museum, 135 (Pörtner, *Athen und Konstantinopel,* III/10).

Father	*wr mdw šmʿ dd.tw-sbk*
Mother ?	*ẖkrt-nswt ḥpw*

XI/94 ***sbk-ḥtp*** [305/6]
London, BM EA 1163 (*HT* IV, 18-20).

Son	*sš ḥnw-nṯr sbk-ḥtp*
Daughter-in-law	*ẖkrt-nswt iwḥt-ib*

XI/95 ***sbk-ṯ3w.s*** [-]
Chiddingston Castle, EDECC:01.2882 (Grajetzki, in: *IBAES* V, 62-65)

Mother	*ẖkrt-nswt sm-ib*
Father	*iry-pʿt ḥ3ty-ʿ s3b sḥḏ sš s3-imn*
Brothers	*3ṯw n tt ḥḳ3 s3-imn / rs*
	wr mḏw šmʿ imny-šry
	wr mḏw šmʿ wḏ-h3w
Sisters	*ẖkrt-nswt nbt-m-///*
	ẖkrt-nswt ẖnswt
	ẖkrt-nswt nbw-ḥtp.ty
	ẖkrt-nswt nbw-mtr

XI/96 ***sm-ib*** [-]
Chiddingston Castle, EDECC:01.2882 (Grajetzki, in: *Genealogie. Realität und Fiktion von Identität*, 62-65).

Husband	*iry-pʿt ḥ3ty-ʿ s3b sḥḏ sš s3-imn*
Sons	*3ṯw n tt ḥḳ3 s3-imn / rs*
	wr mḏw šmʿ imny-šry
	wr mḏw šmʿ wḏ-h3w
Daughters	*ẖkrt-nswt nbt-m-///*
	ẖkrt-nswt ẖnswt
	ẖkrt-nswt nbw-ḥtp.ty
	ẖkrt-nswt nbw-mtr
	ẖkrt-nswt sbk-ṯ3w.s
Grandson	*s3-nswt sbk-ḥtp*

XI/97 ***sn-ʿnḫ*** [308/14]
Liverpool, M 14001 (Edwards, *RT* 10, 1888, 132/IV).

Husband	*ꜣṯw n* [*ṯt ḥḳꜣ* ?] *sbk-ḥtp*[316]
Son	*sꜣb ʿnḫ.f*

XI/98 ***snb*** [312/7]
Chiddingston Castle, EDECC:01.2882 (Grajetzki, in: *IBAES* V, 62-65).

Father	*sš wr n mr ḫtmt sꜣ-imn*
Mother	*nbt-pr rn-snb*
Brother	*iry-pʿt ḥꜣty-ʿ sꜣb sḥḏ sš sꜣ-imn*

XI/99 ***snb.s-ʿnḫ.s*** [314/16]
Wien, KHM ÄS 180 (Hein – Satzinger, *Stelen des Mittleren Reiches* I, 103-110).

Husband	*sꜣb r nḫn ḫnsw*[317]

XI/100 ***skt*** [329/7]
Cairo, JdE 48238 (Martin, *Seals*, 1314).

Son	*sꜣ-nswt sꜣ-ḥtḥr*

XI/101 ***di-nwt*** [398/9]
Karlsruhe, Badisches Landesmuseum, H.412 (Spiegelberg-Pörtner, *AG* I, 4 [5]).

Husband	*sš ḏʿtt sš ḥwt-nṯr sn.i-rs*

XI/102 ***dwḥw*** [-]
Cairo, CG 1588 (Borchardt, *Denkmäler des AR* II, 66-67).

Husband	*ḥꜣty-ʿ ḫtmty-bity smr wʿty mr mšʿ idi*

XI/103 ***dtt*** ? [-]
Beni Hasan, Tomb 861 (Garstang, *Burial Customs*, 242, pl. VII).

XI/104 ***dtt-inpt*** ? [-]
Beni Hasan Tomb 800 (Garstang, *Burial Customs*, 240, pl. VII).

---

[316] Cf. Franke, *Doss.*, 578.
[317] Cf. Franke, *Doss.*, 463.

XI/105 ***kwms*** [-]

1) London, BM EA 833 (+ Paris, Louvre E 6167) (Clère, *JEA* 68, 1982, 60-68).

2) Paris, Louvre C 287 [E.13057] (Franke, *JEA* 71, 1985, 175-6 pl. xix).

* *iryt-pꜥt*

Husband	*sš ḥtpw-nṯr wp-wꜣwt-iry*
Son	*ḥꜣty-ꜥ mr ḥwt-nṯr sꜣ-nswt ṯsw iwꜥy n ꜣbḏw kwms*

XI/106 *///*[318]

Cambridge, Fitzwilliam Museum E. 67.1932 (Bourriau, *Pharaohs and Mortals*, no 37).

---

[318] Wrongly described as king's sister.

LIST OF SOURCES

BIBLIOGRAPHY

Abdalla, *JEA* 78, 1992

Abdalla, A. O., The Cenotaph of the Sekwaskhet Family from Saqqara, ***JEA*** 78, 1992, 93-111.

AIB

Aegyptische Inschriften aus den Königlichen / Staatlichen Museen zu Berlin I-II, Leipzig 1913-1924.

Allen, *Field Museum Stelae*

Allen, T. G., *Egyptian Stelae in the Field Museum Natural History*, Chicago 1936.

Alliot, *Tell Edfou*

Alliot, M., *Rapport sur les Fouilles de Tell Edfou (1933)*, FIFAO 10/2, Cairo 1935.

Altenmüller, *Welt des Orients* 14, 1983

Altenmüller, H., Ein Zaubermesser aus Tübingen, ***Welt des Orients*** 14, 1983, 30-45

AJSLL

The American Journal of Semitic Languages and Literature, Chicago.

Andreu, *BIFAO* 80, 1980

Andreu, G., La stèle Louvre C 249: Un complément à la reconstruction d'une chapelle Abydénienne, ***BIFAO*** 80, 1980, 139- 147, pl. xxxviii-xxxix

Andreu, *BSAK* 4, 1990

Andreu, G., Recherches sur la classe moyenne au Moyen Empire, ***BSAK*** 4, 1991, 15-26.

ANOC

Simpson, W. K., *The Terrace of the Great God at Abydos: The Offering Chapels of Dynasties 12 and 13*, New Haven-Philadelphia 1974.

Arnold, *Complex of Senwosret I*

Arnold, D., The Pyramid Complex of Senwosret I, New York 1992.

Arnold, *EA* 9, 1996

Arnold, D., Two New Mastabas of the Twelfth Dynasty at Dahshur, ***EA*** 9, 1996, 23-25.

Arnold, *Tomb Architecture at Lisht*

Arnold, D., *Middle Kingdom Tomb Architecture at Lisht*, New York – New Haven 2009.

ASAE

*Annales du Service des Antiquités de l'Égypt*e, Kairo

Assmann, in: *Lexikon der Ägyptologie* II

Assmann, J., Harfnerlieder, in: ***Lexikon der Ägyptologie*** II, 972-978

Awad, *GM* 197, 2003

Awad, K. A. H., Eine Stele des Mittleren Reiches im Louvre, ***GM*** 197, 2003, 43-48.

Baines, *JEA* 72, 1986

Baines, J., The Stela of Emhab: Innovation, Tradition, Hierarchy, ***JEA*** 72, 1986, 41-53.

Baines, *Visual and written*

Baines, J., *Visual and Written Culture in Ancient Egypt*, Oxford 2007

Ball, ***Light From the East***

Ball, C.J., *Light From the East or, The Witness of the Monuments*, London 1899.

Ben-Tor, *The Israel Museum Journal* 7, 1988

Ben-Tor, D., Scarabs Bearing Titles and Private Names of Officials, ***The Israel Museum Journal*** 7, 1988, 38

Bennett, *GM* 151, 1996

Bennett, C., The King's Daughter Reditenes, ***GM*** 151, 1996, 19-22.

Berlev, *JEA* 60, 1974

Berlev, O., A Contemporary of King Sewah-en-re, ***JEA*** 60, 1974, 106-113.

Берлев, *Общественные отношения*

Берлев, О., *Общественные отношения в Египте эпохи Среднего царства*, Москва 1978.

Берлев, in: *Проблемы социальных отношений*

Берлев, О., Древнейшее описание социальной организации Египта, in: *Проблемы социальных отношений и форм зависимости на древнем Востоке*, Москва 1984, 23-33.

Берлев, *ПС* 17, 1967
Берлев, О, Египетский военный флот в эпоху Среднего царства, ***ПС*** 17, 1967, 6-19.

Берлев, *ПС* 25, 1974, 26-31
Берлев, О. Д., Стела Вюрцбургского унивреситетского музея (XIII династия), ***ПС*** 25, 1974, 26-31.

Berlev, *RdÉ* 23, 1971
Berlev, O., Les prétendus "citadins" au Moyen Empire, ***RdÉ*** 23, 1971, 23-48.

Берлев, О., *Trudovoe*
Берлев, *Трудовое население Египта в эпоху Среднего царства*, Москва 1972.

BIFAO
*Bulletin de l'Institut Français d'Archéologie Oriental*e, Kairo.

Björkman, *Linköping Museum*
Björkman, G., *A Selection of the Objects in the Smith Collection of Egyptian Antiquities*, Uppsala 1971.

Blackman, *Meir*
Blackman, A. M., *The Rock Tombs of Meir I-VI*, London 1914-1953.

Boeser, *Leiden* II
Boeser, P.A.A. *Beschrijving van de Egyptische verzameling in het Rijksmuseum van Oudheden te Leiden. De monumenten van den tijd tusschen het Oude en het Middelrijk en van het Middelrijk. Eerste afdeeling: Stèles*, Gravenhage 1909.

Borchardt, *Denkmäler des AR*
Borchardt, L., *Denkmäler des Alten Reiches*, Le Caire 1961.

Bostico, *Le Stele Egiz.*
Bostico, S., *Museo Archeologico di Firenze. Le Stele egiziane dall'antico al nuovo regno*, Rome 1959.

Botti, *Museo dell' Accademia di Cortona*
Botti G., *Le antichita egiziane del Museo dell' Accademia di Cortona ordinate e descritte*, Firenze 1955.

Bourriau, *Pharaohs and Mortals*

Bourriau, J., *Pharaohs and Mortals*, Cambridge 1988.

Brack, *SAK* 11, 1984

Brack, A. 'Diskussionsbeitrag zu dem Titel Xkrt njswt', ***SAK*** 11, 1984, 183-186

Brunner-Traut, *Die Ägyptische Sammlung der Universität Tübingen*

Brunner-Traut, E. - Brunner, H., *Die Ägyptische Sammlung der Universität Tübingen*, I-II, Mainz am Rhein 1981.

Bryan, in: *Mistress of the House, Mistress of Heaven*

Bryan, B. M., In woman good and bad fortune are on earth: status and roles of women in Egyptian culture, in: *Mistress of the House, Mistress of Heaven: Women in Ancient Egypt*, ed. by A. K. Capel and G. E. Markoe, New York 1996, 25-46.

BSAK

Studien zur Altägyptischen Kultur, Beihefte, Hamburg.

Budge, *Egyptian Antiquities in the possession of Lady Meux*

Budge, W., *Some Account of the Collection of Egyptian Antiquities in the possession of Lady Meux of Theobalds Park, Waltham Cross.*, London 1893.

Burt, *BIFAO* 107, 2008

Burt, K. 'La condition des nourrices sous le Moyen Empire', ***BIFAO*** 107, 2008, 109-126.

Černy, *IS*

Gardiner, A., Peet, T.E., Černy J., *The Inscriptions of Sinai*, vol. I – vol. II: Introductions and Plates, London 1952-1955.

Černý, *JEA* 31, 1945

Černý, J., The Will of Naunakhte and the related Documents, ***JEA*** 31, 1945, 29-53.

Catalogue of the Amherst Collection

Catalogue of the Amherst Collection of Egyptian & Oriental antiquities [13–17 June, 1921], London 1921.

CdÉ

*Chronique d'Égypt*e, Brüssel.

Chevereau, *RdÉ* 43, 1992

Chevereau, P.-M., Contribution à la prosopographie des cadres militaires du Moyen Empire: Titres nautiques, ***RdÉ*** 43, 1992, 11-34.

Clère, *JEA* 68, 1982

Clère, J.J., La stele de Sânkhptah, chambellan du roi Râhotep, ***JEA*** 68, 1982, 60-68.

Clère, *RdÉ* 7, 1949

Clère, J.J., La Stèled'un commissaire de police (mr-Snt) de la Première période intermédiaire, ***RdÉ*** 7, 1949, 19-32.

Collier – Quirke, *The UCL Lahun Papyri: Accounts*

Collier, M. – Quirke, S., *The UCL Lahun Papyri: Accounts*, BAR International Series 1471, London 2006.

Collier-Quirke, *The UCL Lahun Papyri: Letters*

Collier, M. - Quirke, S., *The UCL Lahun Papyri: Letters*, Oxford 2002.

Collier-Quirke, *The UCL Lahun Papyri: Religious*

Collier, M. - Quirke, S., *The UCL Lahun Papyri: Religious, literary, legal, mathematical and medical*, Oxford 2004.

Cultes Funéraires en Égypte et en Nubie

Les Cultes Funéraires en Égypte et en Nubie. Catalogue d'exposition - Musées des beaux-arts de Calais, Calais 1988.

Daressy, *ASAE* 17, 1917

Daressy, M. G., Monuments d'Edfou da fant du Moyen Empire, ***ASAE*** 17, 1917, 237-244.

Daressy, *RT* 14, 1893

Daressy, M. G., Remarques et notes, ***RT*** 14, 1893, 20-38.

Davies, *Antefoker*

Davies, N. de G. – Gardiner, A., *The Tomb of Antefoker*, London 1920

Delange, *Cat. statues ég. M. E.*

Delange, E., *Musée du Louvre. Catalogue des statues égyptiennes du Moyen Empire, 2060–1560 avant J.-C.*, Paris 1987.

DeM

De Morgan, J., *Catalogue des Monuments et Inscriptions de l'Égypte antique I, De la Frontière de Nubie à Kom Ombos*, Wien 1894.

Dolzani, in: *Viaggatori veneti alla scoperta dell'Egitto*

Dolzani, C., Antichità Egizie in Padova, in: *Viaggatori veneti alla scoperta dell'Egitto*, ed. by A. Siliotti, Venezia 1985.

Downes, *Excavations Esna 1905-1906*

Downes, D., *The Excavations at Esna 1905-1906*, Warminster 1974.

Doxey, *Non-royal Epithets*

Doxey, D., *Egyptian Non-royal Epithets in the Middle Kingdom. A Social and Historical Analysis,* Leiden 1998

Drenkhahn, *SAK* 4, 1976

Drenkhahn, R., 'Bemerkungen zu dem Titel Xkr.t nswt', ***SAK*** 4, 1976, 59-67

Dunham - Janssen, *SCF* II

Dunham, D. – Janssen. J., *Second Cataract Forts, vol. II: Uronarti, Shalfak, Mirgissa*, Boston 1967.

Dyroff-Pörtner, *AG* II

Dyroff, K. – Pörtner, B., *Aegyptische Grab und Denksteine aus süddeutschen Sammlungen* II, Strassburg 1904.

EA

Egyptian archaeology, London.

Edwards, *JEA* 51, 1965

Edwards, I. E. S., Lord Dufferin's Excavations at Deir el-Bahari, ***JEA*** 51, 1965, 16-28

Edwards, *RT* 10, 1888

Edwards, I. E. S., The provincial and private collections of Egyptian antiquities in Great Britain, ***RT*** 10, 1888, 121-133.

Emerit, *BIFAO* 102, 2002

Emerit, S., À propos de l'origine des interdits musicaux dans l'Égypte ancienne, ***BIFAO*** 102, 2002, 189-210.

Engelbach, *ASAE* 22, 1922

Engelbach, R., Steles and Tables of Offerings of the Late Middle Kingdom from Tell Edfu, ***ASAE*** 22, 1922, 113-123.

Eyre, *JEA* 93, 2007

Eyre, C.J., The evil stepmother and the rights of a second wife, ***JEA*** 93, 2007, 223-243.

Eyre, in: *Le commerce en Égypte ancienne*

Eyre, C.J., The market women of pharaonic Egypt, in: N. Grimal and P. Menu (eds.), *Le commerce en Égypte ancienne*, Cairo 1998, 173-192.

Fantechi - Zingarelli, *GM* 186, 2002

Fantechi E.S. - Zingarelli, A. P., Singers and Musicians in New Kingdom Egypt, *GM* 186, 2002, 27-35.

Faulkner, *Coffin Texts* I

Faulkner, R. O., *The Ancient Egyptian Coffin Texts* I, Warminster 1973.

Fekri, in: *Studies in honor of Ali Radwan. Vol. 1*

Fekri, M.M., 'Les protectrices de la famille royale 'Khekerout Nesout' dans l'Égypte ancienne', in: K.A. Daoud (ed.), *Studies in honor of Ali Radwan. Vol. 1*, Le Caire 2005, 353-374.

Feucht, *Das Kind im Alten Ägypten*

Feucht, E., *Das Kind im Alten Ägypten. Die Stellung des Kindes in Familie und Gesellschaft nach altägyptischen Texten und Darstellungen*, Frankfurt - New York 1995.

Fischer, *Egyptian Titles of the Middle Kingdom*

Fischer, H. G., *Egyptian Titles of the Middle Kingdom. A Supplement to Wm. Ward's Index*, New York 1985.

Fischer, *Egyptian Studies I*

Fischer, H.G., *Egyptian Studies I. Varia*, New York 1976.

Fischer, *Egyptian Studies III*

Fischer, H. G., *Egyptian Studies III. Varia Nova*, New York 1996.

Fischer, *Egyptian Women*

Fischer, H.G., *Egyptian Women of the Old Kingdom and of the Heracleopolitan Period,* New York 1989.

Fischer, *JNES* 16, 1957

Fischer, H. G., A God and a General of the Oasis on a Stela of the Late MK, ***JNES*** 16, 1957, 223-235.

Franke, *AVB*

Franke, D., *Altägyptische Verwandtschaftsbezeichnungen im Mittleren Reich*, Hamburg 1983.

Franke, *Doss.*

Franke, D., *Personendaten aus dem Mittleren Reich (20.-16. Jahrhundert v. Chr.). Dossiers 1-796*, Wiesbaden 1984.

Franke, *Heqaib*
Franke, D., *Das Heiligtum des Heqaib auf Elephantine*, Heidelberg 1994

Franke, *JEA* 71, 1985
Franke, D., An important family from Abydos of the Seventeenth Dynasty, ***JEA*** 71, 1985, 175-176.

Franke, *JEA* 76, 1990
Franke, D., Ward, W., *Essays on Feminine Titles of the Middle Kingdom and Related Subjects*, Beirut 1986. (Review), ***JEA*** 76, 1990, 228-232.

Franke, in: *Middle Kingdom Studies*
Franke, D. The career of Khnumhotep III of Beni Hasan and the so-called "decline of the nomarchs", in: *Middle Kingdom Studies*, ed. by S. Quirke, New Malden 1991, 51-68.

Franke, *MDAIK* 57, 2001
Franke, D., Drei neue Stelen des Mittleren Reiches von Elephantine, ***MDAIK*** 57, 2001, 15-33.

Franke, in: *Miscellanea Aegyptologica*
Franke, D., Anchu. der Gefolgsmann des Prinzen, in: *Miscellanea Aegyptologica, W. Helck zum 75. Geburtstsag,* Hrsg. H. Altenmüller, R. Germer, Hamburg 1989, 67-87.

Franke, *SAK* 10, 1983
Franke, D. Die Stele Inv. Nr. 4403 im Landesmuseum in Oldenburg, ***SAK*** 10, 1987, 157-178.

Franke, in: *Studies Assman*, 123.
Franke, D., Middle Kingdom Hymns and Other Sundry Religious Texts – An Inventory, in: Egypt: Temple of the Whole World. Studies in Honour of Jan Assman, ed. by S. Meyer, 2003, 95-134.

Frankfort, *JEA* 14, 1928
Frankfort, H., The Cemeteries of Abydos: Work of the Season 1925-26, ***JEA*** 14, 1928, 235-245.

Freed, in: *Studies Simpson* I
Freed, R. E., Stela Workshops of Early Dynasty 12, in: *Studies in Honor of William Kelly Simpson*, Boston 1996, 297-336.

Galvin, *Priests and Priestesses of Hathor*

Galvin, M., *Priests and Priestesses of Hathor in the Old Kingdom and First Intermediate Period*, PhD. Diss., Brandeis University 1981 (unpublished).

Galvin, *JEA* 70, 1984

Galvin, M., The Hereditary Status of the Titles of the Cult of Hathor, ***JEA*** 70, 1984, 42-49

Gardiner, *AEO*

Gardiner, A. H., *Ancient Egyptian Onomastica*. 3 vols. Oxford 1947.

Gardiner, *Sinuhe*

Gardiner, A. H., *Notes on the Story of Sinuhe*, Paris 1916.

Gardiner, *Wilbour Papyrus*

Gardiner, A. H. (ed.), *The Wilbour Papyrus,* Vol. II, Oxford 1948.

Gardiner - Sethe, *Letters to the Dead*

Gardiner, A. H. - Sethe, K. H., *Egyptian Letters to the Dead,* London 1928.

Garstang, *El-Arabah*

Garstang, J., *El-Arabah*, London 1900.

Garstang, *Burial Customs*

Garstang, J., *The Burial Customs of Ancient Egypt as Illustrated by Tombs of the Middle Kingdom*, London 1907.

Gautier-Jequier, *Fouilles de Licht*

Gautier, J.-E. - Jequier, G., *Memoire sur les fouilles de Licht*, MIFAO VI, Le Caire 1902.

Gayet, *Stèles de la XIIe dyn.*

Gayet, A. J., *Stèles de la XIIe Dynastie*, Paris 1889.

Gillam, *JARCE* 32, 1995

Gillam, R., Priestesses of Hathor: Their Function, Decline, and Disappearance, ***JARCE*** 32, 1995, 211-237.

GM

Göttinger Miszellen, Göttingen.

Goyon, *Ouadi Hammamat*

Goyon, G., *Nouvelles Inscriptions rupestres du Ouadi Hammamat*, Paris 1957.

Graefe, *Gottesgemahlin des Amun*

Graefe, E., Untersuchungen zur Verwaltung und Geschichte der Institutionder Gottesgemahlin des Amun vom Beginn des Neuen Reiches bis zur Spätzeit, Wiesbaden 1981.

Grajetzki, in: *IBAES* V

Grajetzki, W., Zwei Fallbeispiele für Genalogien im Mittleren Reich, in: *Genealogie. Realität und Fiktion von Identität. IBAES* V, Hrgr. von Martin Fitzenreiter, London 2005, 62-65.

Grajetzki, *Two Treasurers*

Grajetzki, W., *Two Treasurers of the late Middle Kingdom*, London 2001

Grajetzki, *Zentralverwaltung*

Grajetzki, W., *Die Höchsten Beamten der ägyptischen Zentralverwaltung zur Zeit des Mittleren Reiches*, Berlin 2000.

Graves-Brown, in: *Sex and Gender in Ancient Egypt*

Graves-Brown, C. Gender, Sex and Loss of Innocence, in: Sex and Gender in Ancient Egypt, ed. by C. Graves-Brown, The Classical Press of Wales 2008, ix-xxv.

Grdseloff, *JEA* 35, 1949

Grdseloff, B., A New Middle Kingdom Letter from El-Lāhūn, ***JEA*** 35, 1949, 59-62.

Griffith-Newberry, *El Bersheh*

Griffith, F. L. - Newberry, P. E., *El Bersheh* I-II, London 1895.

Habachi, *Elephantine* IV

Habachi, L., *Elephantine* IV*: The Sanctuary of Heqaib*, Mainz am Rhein 1985.

Hagen, *ZÄS* 135, 2008

Hagen, F., A Ramesside Administrative Document (P. Cambridge University Library MS. Add. 4167), ***ZÄS*** 135, 2008, 30-39.

Hannig, *Ägyptisches Wörterbuch* II

Hannig, R., *Ägyptisches Wörterbuch* II. *Mittleres Reich und Zweite Zwischenzeit*, Mainz am Rhein 2006

Hayes, *JEA* 33, 1947

Hayes, W. C., Horemkhauef of Nekhen and his Trip to It-towe, ***JEA*** 33, 1947, 3-11.

Hayes, *Papyrus Brooklyn*

Hayes, W. C., *A Papyrus of the Late Middle Kingdom in the Brooklyn Museum*, Brooklin 1972.

Hayes, *The Scepter of Egypt* I

Hayes, W. C., *The Scepter of Egypt I. From the Earliest Times to the End of the Middle Kingdom*, New York 1955.

Hein – Satzinger, *Stelen des Mittleren Reiches*

Hein I. –Satzinger, H., *Stelen des Mittleren Reiches I, einschließlich der I. und II Zwischenzeit,* CAA, Kunshistorisches Museum Wien 4, Mainz 1989.

Hein I. –Satzinger, H., *Stelen des Mittleren Reiches II, einschließlich der I. und II Zwischenzeit,* CAA, Kunshistorisches Museum Wien 7, Mainz 1993.

Helck, *Militärführer in der 18. ägyptischen Dynastie*

Helck,W., *Der Einfluss der Militärführer in der 18. ägyptischen Dynastie*, Leipzig 1939.

Helck, *Verwaltung*

Helck, W. *Zur Verwaltung des Mittleren und Neuen Reiches*, Leiden 1975.

Hodjash - Berlev, *Pushkin Museum*

Hodjash S. - Berlev, O., *The Egyptian Reliefs and Stelae in the Pushkin Museum of Fine Arts,* Moscow-Leningrad 1982.

Hofmann, *b3k* und *ḥm*

Hofmann, T., Zur sozialen Bedeutung zweier Begriffe für <Diener>: *b3k* und *ḥm*, Basel 2005.

Hofmann, in: *Living and Writing in Deir el-Medina*

Hofmann, T., Arbeitseinsätze und Löhne der sogenannten Sklavinnen von Deir el-Medine, in: *Living and Writing in Deir el-Medina. Socio-historical Embodiment of Deir el-Medine Texts*, ed. by A. Dorn and T. Hofmann, Basel 2006, 113-118.

HT

Hall, H.R., Lambert, E.J., Scott-Moncrieff, P.D., *Hieroglyphic Texts from Egyptian Stelae etc. in the British Museum* II, London 1912.

Hall, H.R., Lambert, E.J., *Hieroglyphic Texts from Egyptian Stelae etc. in the British Museum* III, London 1912.
Hall, H.R., Lambert, E.J., *Hieroglyphic Texts from Egyptian Stelae etc. in the British Museum* IV, London 1913.
Hall, H.R., Lambert, E.J., *Hieroglyphic Texts from Egyptian Stelae etc. in the British Museum* V, London 1914.
Hall, H.R., Lambert, E.J., *Hieroglyphic Texts from Egyptian Stelae etc. in the British Museum* VI, London 1922.

Jacquet-Gordon, *Karnak-Nord* VIII
Jacquet-Gordon, H., *Karnak-Nord* VIII. *Le Trésor de Thoutmosis Ier. Statues, Stèles et Blocs Réutilisés*. FIFAO 39, Le Caire 1999.

James, *Corpus of Hieroglyphic Inscriptions* I
James, T. G. H., *Corpus of Hieroglyphic Inscriptions in The Brooklyn Museum I: From Dynasty I to the End of Dynasty XVIII*, Brooklyn 1971

Janssen, in: *Studies Wente*
Janssen, J., A Marital Title from the New Kingdom, in: *Gold of Praise. Studies on Ancient Egypt in Honor of E. F. Wente*, ed. by E. Teeter and J. A. Larson, Chicago – Illinois 1999, 185-192.

JARCE
Journal of the American Research Center in Egypt, Cairo.

JEA
Journal of Egyptian Archaeology, London.

JNES
Journal of Near Eastern Studies, Chicago.

Johnson, in: *The Life of Meresamun*
Johnson, J. H., The Societal, Economic, and Legal Status of Women in Ancient Egypt, in: *The Life of Meresamun. A Temple Singer in Ancient Egypt,* ed. by E. Teeter and J. H. Johnson, Chicago 2009, 82-91.

Johnson, in: *Mistress of the House, Mistress of Heaven*
Johnson, J. H., The Legal Status of Women in Ancient Egypt in: *Mistress of the House, Mistress of Heaven: Women in Ancient Egypt*, ed. by A. K. Capel and G. E. Markoe, New York 1996, 175-86 and 215-218.

Johnson, in: *Studies Quaegebeur*

Johnson, J. H., Women, Wealth and Work in Egyptian Society of the Ptolemaic Period, in: *Egyptian Religion, The Last Thousand Years, Studies Dedicated to the Memory of Jan Quaegebeur*, ed. by W. Clarysse, A. Schoors, and H. Willems, Leuven 1998, 1393-1421.

Jones, *Index of Ancient Egyptian Titles*

Jones, D., *An Index of Ancient Egyptian Titles, Epithets and Phrases of the Old Kingdom* I-II, Oxford 2000.

Kaiser, *Äegyptisches Museum Berlin*

Kaiser, W., *Äegyptisches Museum Berlin*, Berlin 1967.

Kaiser, *MDAIK* 28, 1972

Kaiser, W, Stadt und Tempel von Elephantine. Driter Grabungsbericht, ***MDAIK*** 28, 1972, 157-200.

Kamal, *ASAE* 4, 1903

Kamal, A. B. Fouilles a Tehneh, ***ASAE*** 4, 1903, 232-241.

Kamal, *Tables d'offrandes*

Kamal, A. B., *Tables d'offrandes CGC 23001-23256*, Cairo 1909.

Katary, in: *Agriculture in Egypt*

Katary, S. L. D., Land-Tenure in the New Kingdom: The Role of Women Smallholders and the Military, in: *Agriculture in Egypt*, ed. by A. K. Bowman and E. Rogan, Oxford 1998, 61-82.

Katary, *Land Tenure*

Katary, S. L. D., *Land Tenure in the Ramesside Period*, London-New York, 1989.

Koefoed-Petersen, *Stele eg. Copenhague*

Koefoed-Petersen, O., *Les Stèles égyptiennes. Publications de la Glyptothèque Ny Carlsberg,* Copenhague 1948.

Kóthay, *Acta Antiqua Academiae Scientiarum Hungaricae* 46, 2006

Kóthay, K. A., The Widow and Orphan in Egypt before the New Kingdom, *Acta Antiqua Academiae Scientiarum Hungaricae* 46, 2006, 151-164.

Krah, *Die Harfe im pharaonischen Ägypten*

Krah, K., *Die Harfe im pharaonischen Ägypten: Ihre Entwicklung und Funktion*, Göttingen 1991

Lacau, *Sarcophages*

Lacau, P., *Sarcophages antérieurs au nouvel empire.* 2Bde, Cairo 1904-1906.

Lange-Schäfer, *CGC* I-II

Lange, H.O. - Schäfer, H., *Grab- und Denksteine des Mittleren Reiches im Museum von Kairo. No. 20001-20780.* I-II, Berlin 1902-1908.

Lapp, *MDAIK* 50, 1991

Lapp, G., Die Stelenkapelle des Kmz aus der 13. Dynastie, ***MDAIK*** 50, 1991, 231-252, Tf. 37-41.

Ledrain, *Les Monuments Égyptiens*

Ledrain, E., *Les Monuments Égyptiens de la Bibliothèque Nationale*, Paris 1879.

Legrain, *RT* 24, 1902

Legrain, G. Le temple et les chapelles d'Osiris a Karnak, ***RT*** 24, 1902, 213.

Leprohon, *Stelae* I

Leprohon, R. J., *Boston Museum of Fine Arts, Stelae 1,The Early Dynastic Period to the Late Middle Kingdom*, fasc. 2, Corpus Antiquitatum Aegyptiacarum, Mainz 1985.

Lesko, in: *Studies Wente*

Lesko, B., 'Listening' to the Ancient Egyptian Woman: Letters, Testimonials, and Other Expressions of Self, in: *Gold of Praise: Studies on Ancient Egypt in Honor of Edward F. Wente*, ed. by E. Teeter and J. A. Larson, Chicago 1999, 247-254.

Lesko, *Women's earliest records*

Lesko. B., (ed.) *Women's earliest records from ancient Egypt and Western Asia*, Atlanta 1989.

LD

Lepsius, K. R., *Denkmaeler aus Aegypten und Aethiopien*, 12 Bdc., Berlin 1849-1858.

Lichtheim, *JNES* 4, 1945

Lichtheim, M., The Songs of the Harpers, ***JNES*** 4, 1945, 178-212.

Liebieghaus Museum. Ägyptische Bildwerke III

Liebieghaus Museum Alter Plastik, Wissenschaftliche Kataloge. Ägyptische Bildwerke III: Skulptur, Malerei, Papyri und Särge, H. Beck (Hrg.), Frankfurt am Main 1993.

Lorenz, in: *The Life of Meresamun*

Lorenz, M, Women and Their Employment, in: *The Life of Meresamun. A Temple Singer in Ancient Egypt,* ed. by E. Teeter and J. H. Johnson, Chicago 2009, 98-101.

Luft, *ZÄS* 115, 1988

Luft, U. Eine Stele des späten Mittleren Reiches in Krakau, ***ZÄS*** 115, 1988, 147-153.

Lustig, in: *Anthropology and Egyptology*

Lustig, J., Gender and Age in Middle Kingdom Tomb Scenes and Text, in: *Anthropology and Egyptology*, ed. by J. Lustig, Schefield 1997, 43-65.

Lutz, *Tomb Steles*

Lutz, H. F., *Egyptian Tomb Steles and Offering Stones,* Leipzig 1927.

Manniche, *Music and Musicians*

Manniche, L., *Music and Musicians in Ancient Egypt*, London 1991

Markoe - Capel, *Mistress of the House, Mistress of Heaven*

Markoe G. E. - Capel, A. K., *Mistress of the House, Mistress of Heaven: Women in Ancient Egypt.* Cincinnati 1996

Martin, *Fitzwilliam Museum*

Martin, G. T., *Stelae from Egypt and Nubia in the Fitzwilliam Museum, Cambridge, c. 3000 BC – AD 1150,* Cambridge 2005.

Martin, *MDAIK* 35, 1979

Martin, G. T., Private-Name Seals in the Alnwick Castle Collection, ***MDAIK*** 35, 1975, 215-226.

Martin, *Seals*

Martin, G. T., *Egyptian Administrative and Private Name Seals Principally of the Middle Kingdom and Second Intermediate Period,* Oxford 1971.

Maspero, *RT* 3, 1882

Maspero, G., Rapport sur une mission en Italie, ***RT*** 3, 1882, 103-127.

Maspero, *RT* 13, 1890

Maspero, G., Monuments égyptiens du Musée de Marseille, ***RT*** 13, 1890, 113-126.

Maspero, *ZÄS* 20, 1882

Maspero, G., Notes sur quelques points de Grammaire et d'Histoire, ***ZÄS*** 20, 1882, 120-135.

MDAIK

Mitteilungen des Deutschen Archäologischen Instituts, Abt. Kairo, Wiesbaden-Mainz.

Meeks, *Alex.*

Meeks, D., *Année Lexicographique. Égypte Ancienne* I-III, Paris 1980-1982.

Meskell, *Archaeologies of Social Life*

Meskell, L., *Archaeologies of Social Life. Age, class et cetera in Ancient Egypt*, Oxford 1999.

Millard, *Position of Women in the Family and in Society*

Millard, A. *The Position of Women in the Family and in Society in Ancient Egypt: with special reference to the Middle Kingdom*. 3 vols. London: University of London 1976 (unpublished).

Mogensen, *Inscriptions Copenhague*

Mogensen, M., *Inscriptions hiéroglyphiques du Musée National de Copenhague*, Kopenhagen 1918.

Montet, *Ouâdi Hammâmât*

Montet, P – Couyat, J., *Les Inscriptions hiéroglyphiques et hiératiques du Ouâdi Hammâmât*, cairo 1912.

Montserrat, *Sex and Society in Graeco-Roman Egypt*

Montserrat, D., *Sex and Society in Graeco-Roman Egypt*. London 1996.

Moret, *Annales du Musee Guimet*

Moret, A., *Catalogue du Musée Guimet. Galerie égyptienne. Annales du Musée Guimet, 32,* Paris 1909.

Morley, *Ancient History*

Morley, N., *Theories, Models and Concepts in Ancient History*, London – New York 2004.

Newberry, *Beni Hasan*

Newberry, P. E., *Beni Hasan* I-II, London 1893-1894.

Newberry, *PSBA* 25, 1903

Newberry, P.E., Extracts from my Notebooks (VI), ***PSBA*** 25, 1903, 130-138.

Noblecourt, *La femme au temps des pharaons*

Noblecourt, C. D., *La femme au temps des pharaons,* Paris 1986.

Nord, *Serapis* 2, 1970

Nord, D., 'Xkrt-nswt = "King's Concubine"?' ***Serapis*** 2, 1970, 1-16.

Nord, in: *Studies in Ancient Egypt, the Aegean, and the Sudan*

Nord, D., The term xnr: "harem" or "musical performers"?, in: *Studies in Ancient Egypt, the Aegean, and the Sudan*, ed. by W. K. Simpson and W. M. Davies, Boston 1981, 137-145.

Northampton, *Theban Necropolis*

Northampton, W. C., Spiegelberg, W., Newberry P.**,** *Report on Some Excavations in the Theban Necropolis During the Winter of 1889-9*, London 1908.

O'Brien, *Women in Demotic Business and Administrative Texts*

O'Brien, A., *Private Tradition, Public State: Women in Demotic Business and Administrative Texts from Ptolemaic and Roman Thebes.* PhD Dissertation. Chicago: The University of Chicago 1999 (unpublished).

Ogdon, *RSUE* 19, 2002

Ogdon, J. R., Observaciones sobre una stela del reino Medio tardío procedente de Abidos (Merseyside County Museum Liverpool 1977.109.36), ***RSUE*** 19, 2002, 7-12

Onstine, *The Role of the Chantress (šmyt)*

Onstine, S. L., *The Role of the Chantress (šmyt) in Ancient Egypt*, London 2005

Orel, in: *Studies Share*

Orel, S. E., The Stela of Khnumhotep in the British Museum (BM 625) in: *The Unbroken reed. Studies in the Culture and Heritage of Ancient Egypt in Honour of A. F. Share*, ed. by C. Eyre, A. Leahy and L. M. Leahy, London 1994, 227-241.

Page-Gasser, *Ägypten*

Page-Gasser, M., *Ägypten - Augenblicke der Ewigkeit unbekannte Schätze aus Schweizer Privatbesitz [Antikenmuseum Basel und Sammlung Ludwig, 18. März - 13. Juli 1997]*, Mainz 1997.

Parkinson, *JEA* 81, 1995

Parkinson, R.B., “Homosexual” desire and Middle Kingdom Literature, ***JEA*** 81, 1995, 57-76.

Parkinson, in: *Sex and Gender in Ancient Egypt*

Parkinson, R.B., Boasting about hardness: constructions of Middle Kingdom masculinity, in: *Sex and Gender in Ancient Egypt*, ed. by C. Graves-Brown, The Classical Press of Wales 2008, 115-142.

Parkinson – Franke, in: *Essays in Honor of David B. O'Connor*

Parkinson, R.B. –Franke, D., A Song for Sarenput: Texts from Qubbet el-Hawa Tomb 36, in: *The Arcahaeology and Art of Ancient Egypt. Essays in Honor of David B. O'Connor*, ed. by Z.A. Hawass and J. Richard, ***ASAE*** Cahier no 36, vol. 2, Le Caire 2007, 219-235.

Patch, *Ancient Egypt*

Patch, D. C., *Reflections of Greatness: Ancient Egypt at The Carnegie Museum of Natural History*, Pittsburgh 1990.

Peet, *Cem. Abydos* II

Peet, T. E., *The Cemeteries of Abydos* II, London 1914.

Peet, *Cem. Abydos* III

Peet, T. E.- Loat, W. L .S., *The Cemeteries of Abydos* III, London 1913.

Pestman, *Marriage and Matrimonial Property*

Pestman, P. W., *Marriage and Matrimonial Property in Ancient Egypt*, Leiden 1961

Petrie, *Abydos I*

Petrie, W. F., *Abydos I*, London 1902.

Petrie, *Abydos II*

Petric, W. F., *Abydos II*, London 1903.

Petrie, *Courtiers*

Petrie, W. M. F., *Tombs of the Courtiers and Oxyrhynkhos*, London 1925.

Petrie, *Qurneh*

Petrie, W. M. F., *Qurneh*, London 1909

Petrie, *Season*

Petrie, W. M. F., *A Season in Egypt 1887*, London 1888.

Petrie - Mace, *Diospolis Parva*

Petrie, W. M. F. - Mace, A.C., *Diospolis Parva: the cemeteries of Abadiyeh and Hu. 1898-9*, London 1901.

Pomeroy, *Women in Hellenistic Egypt*

Pomeroy, S., Women in Hellenistic Egypt: From Alexander to Cleopatra, Detroit 1990.

Pörtner, *Athen und Konstantinopel*

Pörtner, B., *Aegyptische Grabsteine und Denksteine aus Athen und Konstantinopel*, Strassburg 1908.

ПС

Палестинский сборник, Москва

PSBA

Proceedings of the Society of Biblical Archaeology, London.

Quirke, *Administration*

Quirke, S. *The Administration of Egypt in the Late Middle Kingdom*, New Malden 1990.

Quirke, in: *Archaeology and Women*

Quirke, S., Women of Lahun (Egypt 1800 BC), in: S. Hamilton, R.D. Whitehouse and K.I. Wright (eds.), *Archaeology and Women. Ancinet and Modern Issues*, Walnut Creek 2007, 246-262.

Quirke, *Egyptian Literature*

Quirke, S., *Egyptian Literature 1800 BC. Questions and readings*, London 2004.

Quirke, *RdÉ* 37, 1986

Quirke, S., The Regular Titles of the Late Middle Kingdom, ***RdÉ*** 37, 1986, 107-130.

Quirke, in: *Studies in Honour of H. S. Smith*

Quirke, S., Women in Ancient Egypt: Temple Titles and Funerary Papyri, in: *Studies on Ancient Egypt in Honour of H. S. Smith,* ed. by A. Leahy and J. Tait, The Egypt Exploration Society: London 1999, 227-235.

Quirke, *Titles and bureaux*

Quirke, S., *Titles and bureaux of Egypt 1850-1700 BC.*, London. 2004.

Randall-Maciver - Mace, *El Amrah and Abydos*

Randall-Maciver, D. – Mace, A.C., *El Amrah and Abydos 1899-1901*, London 1902.

Ranke, *PN*

Ranke, E., *Die altägyptischen Personennamen*, 2 Bde, Gluckstadt 1935-1952.

Rawson, in: *Women in antiquity*

Rawson, B., From 'daily life' to 'demography, in: *Women in antiquity. New assessments*, ed. by Richard Hawley and Barbara Levick, London and New York 1995, 1-20.

RdÉ

Revue d'Égyptologie, Paris.

Reisner, *Harim*

Reisner, E. *Der königliche Harim in alten Ägypten und seine Verwaltung*, Wien 1972.

Robins, *Women in Ancient Egypt*

Robins, G. *Women in Ancient Egypt*, London 1993.

Roehrig, in: *Mistress of the House, Mistress of Heaven*

Roehrig, C. H., Women's work: Some occupations of nonroyal women as depicted in ancient Egyptian art, in: *Mistress of the House, Mistress of Heaven: Women in Ancient Egypt*, ed. by A. K. Capel and G. E. Markoe, New York 1996, 14-27.

Roehrig, *Royal nurse*

Roehrig, C. H., *The Eighteen Dynasty titles royal nurse (mnˁt nswt), royal tutor (mnˁ nswt), and foster brother/sister of the Ruler of Two Lands (sn/snˁ n mnˁ n nb tȝwy),* PhD Diss., University of California, Berkeley 1996 (unpublished).

Romano, *MDAIK* 48, 1992

Romano, J.F., A Statuette of a Royal Mother and Child in the Brooklyn Museum, ***MDAIK*** 48, 1992, 131-143.

Roth, in: *Companion to the Ancient Near East*

Roth, A. M., Gender Roles in Ancient Egypt, in: *A Companion to the Ancient Near East*, ed. by D. C. Snell, Oxford 2007, 227-234.

RT

Recueil de travaux relatifs à la philologie et à l'archéologie égyptiennes et assyriennes.

Ryholt, *SIP*

Ryholt, K., *The Political Situation in Egypt during the Second Intermediate Period, c. 1800-1550 B.C.*, København 1997.

SAK

Studien zur altägyptischen Kultur, Hamburg.

Scharff, *ZÄS* 57, 1922

Scharff, A., Ein Rechnungsbuch des königlichen Hofes aus der 13. Dynastie (Papyrus Boulaq Nr. 18), ***ZÄS*** 57, 1922, 51-68; 1**-24**.

Schmitz, *Königssohn*

Schmitz, B., Untersuchungen zum Titel s3-njswt "Königssohn", Boon 1976.

Schneider, *Ausländer in Ägypten* II

Schneider, T., *Ausländer in Ägypten während des Mittleren Reiches und der Hyksoszeit. Teil II: Die ausländische Bevölkerung*, Wiesbaden 2003.

Sethe, *Ägyptische Lesestücke*

Sethe, K., *Ägyptische Lesestücke zum Gebrauch im akademischen Unterricht: Texte des Mittleren Reiches*, Leipzig 1928.

Simpson, *JEA* 60, 1974

Simpson, W. K., Polygamy in Egypt in the Middle Kingdom?, ***JEA*** 60, 1974, 100-105.

Smither – Dakin *JEA* 25, 1939

Smither, P. C. – Dakin, A. N., Stelae in the Queen's College, Oxford, ***JEA*** 25, 1939, 157-165.

Spalinger, *RdE* 32, 1980

Spalinger, A., Remarks on the Family of Queen xa.s-nbw and the Problem of Kingship in Dynasty XIII, ***RdE*** 32, 1980, 95-116.

Spalinger, *SAK* 12, 1985

Spalinger, A. J., Notes on the day summary accounts of P.Boulaq 18 and the intradepartmental transfers, ***SAK*** 12, 1985, 179-241.

Spiegelberg-Pörtner, *AG* I

Spiegelberg W. – Pörtner, B., *Aegyptische Grab und Denksteine aus süddeutschen Sammlungen I*, Strassburg 1902.

Stefanović, *GM* 215, 2008

Stefanović, D., The Non-Royal Women of the Middle Kingdom I – *mnꜥt*, ***GM*** 215, 2008, 79-90.

Stefanović, *GM* 218, 2008

Stefanović, D. The Feminine stelae of the Middle Kingdom: Stela Leiden 35, ***GM*** 218, 2008, 81-92.

Stefanović, *GM* 220, 2009

Stefanović, D. The Feminine stelae of the Middle Kingdom: addenda, ***GM*** 220, 2009, 95-98.

Stefanović, *Military Organisation*

Stefanović, D., *The Military Organisation of Pharaonic Egypt in the Period of the Middle Kingdom* (in Serbian), PhD Diss. (unpublished), Belgrade University 2006.

Stefanović, *Military Titles*

Stefanović, D., *The Holders of the Regular Military Titles in the Period of the Middle Kingdom: Dossiers,* London 2006.

Stefanović, in: *Proceedings of the Tenth International Congress of Egyptologists*

Stefanović, D., The *ẖkrt-nswt* on the monuments of the *ꜣṯw n ṯt ḥḳꜣ* in: *Proceedings of the Tenth International Congress of Egyptologists*, ed. by P. Kousoulis (forthcoming).

Stefanović, *SAK* 39, 2009

Stefanović, D. Stela Bolton 1920.10.12. The Non-Royal Women of the Middle Kingdom II - *ẖkrt nswt, bꜣkt nt ḥḳꜣ* and *ꜥnḫt nt tpt nswt*, ***SAK*** 39, 2009 (in print).

Stefanović, *WZKM* 98, 2008,

Stefanović, D., *šmsw* - Soldiers of the Middle Kingdom, ***WZKM*** 98, 2008, 234-248.

Stewart, *Petrie Collection*

Stewart, H. M., *Egyptian Stelae, Reliefs and Paintings from the Petrie Collection*, Warminster 1979.

Sweeney, in: *Living and Writing in Deir el-Medina*

Sweeney, D., Women grooving older in Deir el-Medina, in: *Living and Writing in Deir el-Medina. Socio-historical embodiment of Deir el-Medine texts*, ed. by A. Dorn and T. Hoffmann, Basle 2006, 135-153.

Sweeney, in: *Sesto Congresso Internazionale di Egittologia*

Sweeney, D., Women's correspondence from Deir el-Medineh, in: *Sesto Congresso Internazionale di Egittologia*, Volume 2, Torino 1993, 523-529.

Sweeney, in: *Sex and Gender in Ancient Egypt*

Sweeney, D., Gender and requests in New Kingdom Literature, in: *Sex and Gender in Ancient Egypt*, ed. by C. Graves-Brown, The Classical Press of Wales 2008, 191-214.

Szpakowska, *Daily Life in Ancient Egypt*

Szpakowska, K., *Daily Life in Ancient Egypt. Recreating Lahun*, London, 2008.

Teeter, *Ancient Egypt*

Teeter, E., *Ancient Egypt. Treasures from the Collection of the Oriental Institute University of Chicago*, Chicago 2003.

Teeter, in: *The Life of Meresamun*

Teeter, E., Inside the Temple: The Role and Function of Temple Singers, in: *The Life of Meresamun, A Temple Singer in Ancient Egypt*, ed. by E. Teeter and J. H. Johnson, Chicago 2009, 25-29.

Teeter, in: *Rediscovering the Muses*

Teeter, E., Female Musicians in Pharonic Egypt, in: *Rediscovering the Muses. Women's Musical Tradition,* ed. by K. Marshall, Boston 1993, 68-69.

Toivari-Viitali, *Women at Deir el-Meina*

Toivari-Viitali, J., *Women at Deir el-Meina. A study of the status and roles of the female inhabitants in the workmen's community during the Ramesside Period*, Leiden 2001.

Trapani, in: *Proceedings of the Ninth International Congress of Egyptologists*

Trapani, M., A Prominent Family from Edfu in the Second Intermediate Period (A Study of the Stela CGC 20530 = JdE 22183), in: *Proceedings of the Ninth International Congress of Egyptologists, Grenoble, 6-12 septembre 2004*, ed. by J-C. Goyon and C. Cardin, Leuven 2006, 1827-1838.

Tyldesley, *Daughters of Isis*

Tyldesley, J., *Daughters of Isis. Women in Ancient Egypt*, London 1995.

Tylor, *Tomb of Sebeknekht*

Tylor, J., *Tomb of Sebeknekht at El Kab*, London 1896.

***Urk.* VII**

Sethe, K., *Historisch-biographische Urkunden des Mittleren Reiches*, Leipzig 1935.

Vandekerckhove – Müller-Wollermann, *Eklab* VI

Vandekerckhove, H. –Müller-Wollermann, R., *Eklab VI. Die Felsinschriften des Wadi Hilâl*. I-II, Brepols 2001.

Vandier, *Revue du Louvre* 13, 1963

Vandier, J., Un curieux monument funéraire du Moyen empire, ***Revue du Louvre*** 13, 1963, 1-10.

Vasilika, *Museo Egizio*

Vasilika, E., *Tesori d'arte del Museo Egizio*, Torino 2006.

Vasiljević, *SAK* 24, 1997

Vasiljević, V., Die Herstellung einer Harfe in der Szenen des Holzhandwerks auf Pfeiler XVI des Grabes des Anchtifi in Moala, ***SAK*** 24, 1997, 313-326.

Vasiljević, *SAK*-Beihefte 9, 2003

Vasiljević, V., Die zAgt von Cheti (Beni Hasan Nr.17), *Es werde niedergelegt als Schriftstüch. Festschrift für Hartwig Altenmüller zum 65. Geburtstag*, Hrgs. K. Martin und E. Pardey, *SAK*-Beihefte 9, 2003

Verbovsek, *Private Tempelstatuen*

Verbovsek, A., *«Als Gunsterweis des Königs in den Tempel gegeben...» Private Tempelstatuen des Alten und Mittleren Reiches*, Wiesbaden 2004.

Vernus, *RdÉ* 26, 1974

Vernus, P., Une formule des shaoubtis sur un pseudo-naos de la XIIIe Dynastie, ***RdÉ*** 26, 1974, 101-114.

Ward, *Berytos* 31, 1983

Ward, W., Reflections on some Egyptian terms presumed to mean "Harem, Harem-woman, Concubine", *Berytos* 31, 1983, 67-74.

Ward, *CdÉ* 57, 1982

Ward, W., The at hnqt, "Kitchen", and the Kitchen Staff of Middle Kingdom Private Estates, ***CdÉ*** 57, 1982, 191-200.

Ward, *Feminine Titles*

Ward, W., *Essays on Feminine Titles of the Middle Kingdom and Related Subjects*, Beirut 1986.

Ward, *The Four Egyptian Homographic Roots*

Ward, W., *The Four Egyptian Homographic Roots B-3: Etymological and Egypto-Semitic Studies*, Rome 1978.

Ward, *GM* 71, 1984, 51-59

Ward, W., The Case of Mrs. Tchat and Her Sons in Beni Hasan, ***GM*** 71, 1984, 51-59.

Ward, *Index MK*

Ward, W., *Index of Egyptian Administrative and Religious Titles of the Middle Kingdom*, Beirut 1982.

Ward, in: *Women's Earliest Records*,

Ward, W. A., Non-royal women and the Occupations in the Middle Kingdom, in: *Women's Earliest Records*, ed. by Barbara S. Lesko, Atlanta, 1989, 33-43.

Watterson, *Women in Ancient Egypt.*

Watterson, B., *Women in Ancient Egypt,* Stroud 1991.

Wente, *Letters*

Wente, E. F., *Letters from Ancient Egypt*, Atlanta 1990.

Wiedemann - Pörtner, *AG* III

Wiedemann, A. - Pörtner, B., *Aegyptische Grab und Denksteine aus süddeutschen Sammlungen. Band 3: Bonn, Darmstadt, Frankfurt am Main, Genf, Neuchatel*, Strassburg 1906.

Wiedemann, *PSBA* 9, 1887

Wiedemann, A., On a Relative of Queen Nub-xas, ***PSBA*** 9, 1887, 191.

Wildung, *Sesostris und Amenemhat*

Wildung, D., *Sesostris und Amenemhat. Ägypten im Mittleren Reich*, Munich 1984.

Wilfong, *Women in Ancient Near East*

Wilfong, T.G. *Women in Ancient Near East: A Selected Bibliography of Recent Sources in The Oriental Institute Research Archives*, Chicago: The Oriental Institute Research Archives 1992, oi.uchicago.edu/OI/DEPT/RA/WOMEN.HTML

Willems, *Chests of Life*

Willems, H., *Chests of Life. A Study of the Typology and Conceptual Development of Middle Kingdom Standard Class Coffins*, Leiden 1988.

Willems, *The Coffin of Heqata*

Willems, H. *The Coffin of Heqata (Cairo JdE 36418): A Case Study of Egyptian Funerary Culture of the Early Middle Kingdom*, Leuven 1996.

Willems, *Dayr al-Barsha* I

Willems, H. *Dayr al-Barsha Volume* I. *The Rock Tombs of Djehutinakht (No. 17K74/1), Khnumnakht (No. 17K74/2), and Iha (No. 17K74/3). With an Essay on the History and Nature of Nomarchal Rule in the Early Middle Kingdom*, Leuven 2007.

Winlock, *AJSLL* 57/2, 1940

Winlock, H. E., The Court of King Neb-Hetep-Rē Mentu-Hotpe at the ShaSS er Rigāl, ***AJSLL*** 57/2, 1940, 137-161

Winlock, *Excavations at Deir el Bahari*

Winlock, H. E., *Excavations at Deir el Bahari*, New York 1942.

Winlock, *JEA* 10, 1924

Winlock, H. E., The Tombs of the Kings of the Seventeenth Dynasty at Thebes, ***JEA*** 10, 1924, 217-277.

Winlock, *The Rise and Fall*

Winlock, H. E., *The Rise and Fall of the Middle Kingdom in Thebes*, New York 1947.

WZKM

Wiener Zeitschrift für die Kunde des Morgenlandes, Wien.

ZÄS

Zeitschrift für Ägyptische Sprache und Altertumskunde, Leipzig-Berlin.

Tübingen 459

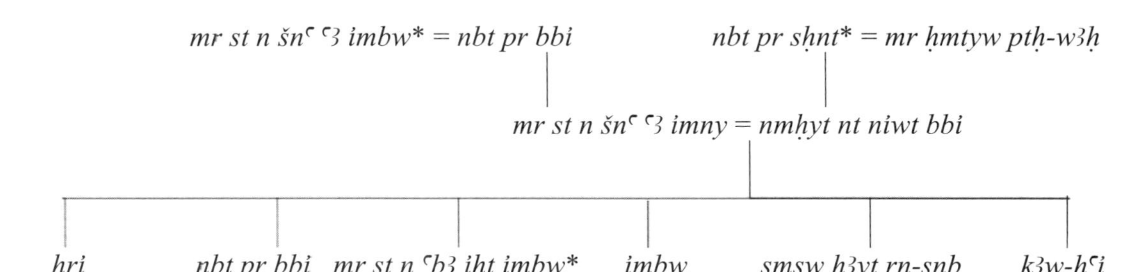

Florence 2553

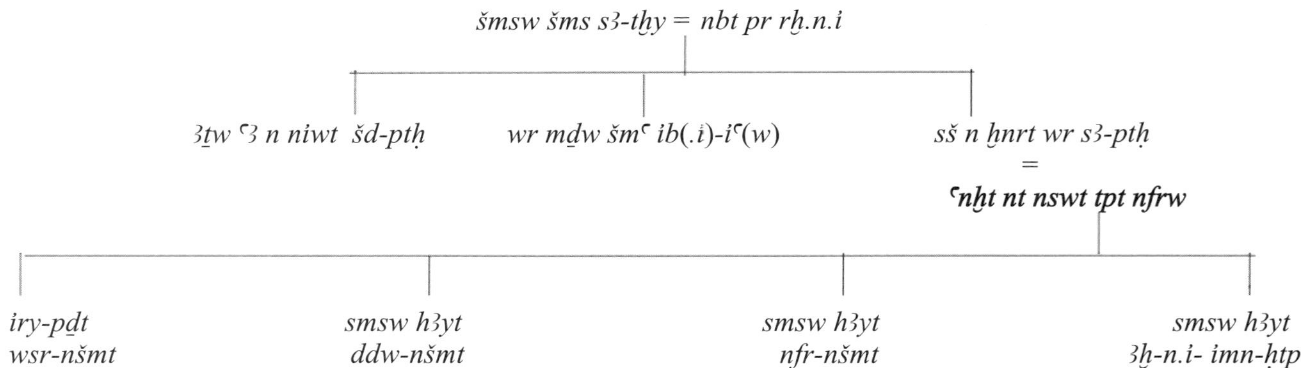

Plate 3

Chiddingston Castle, EDECC:01.2882

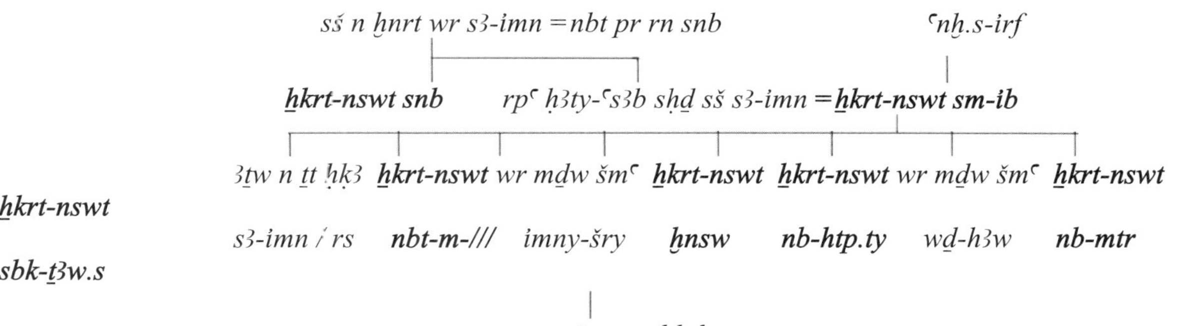

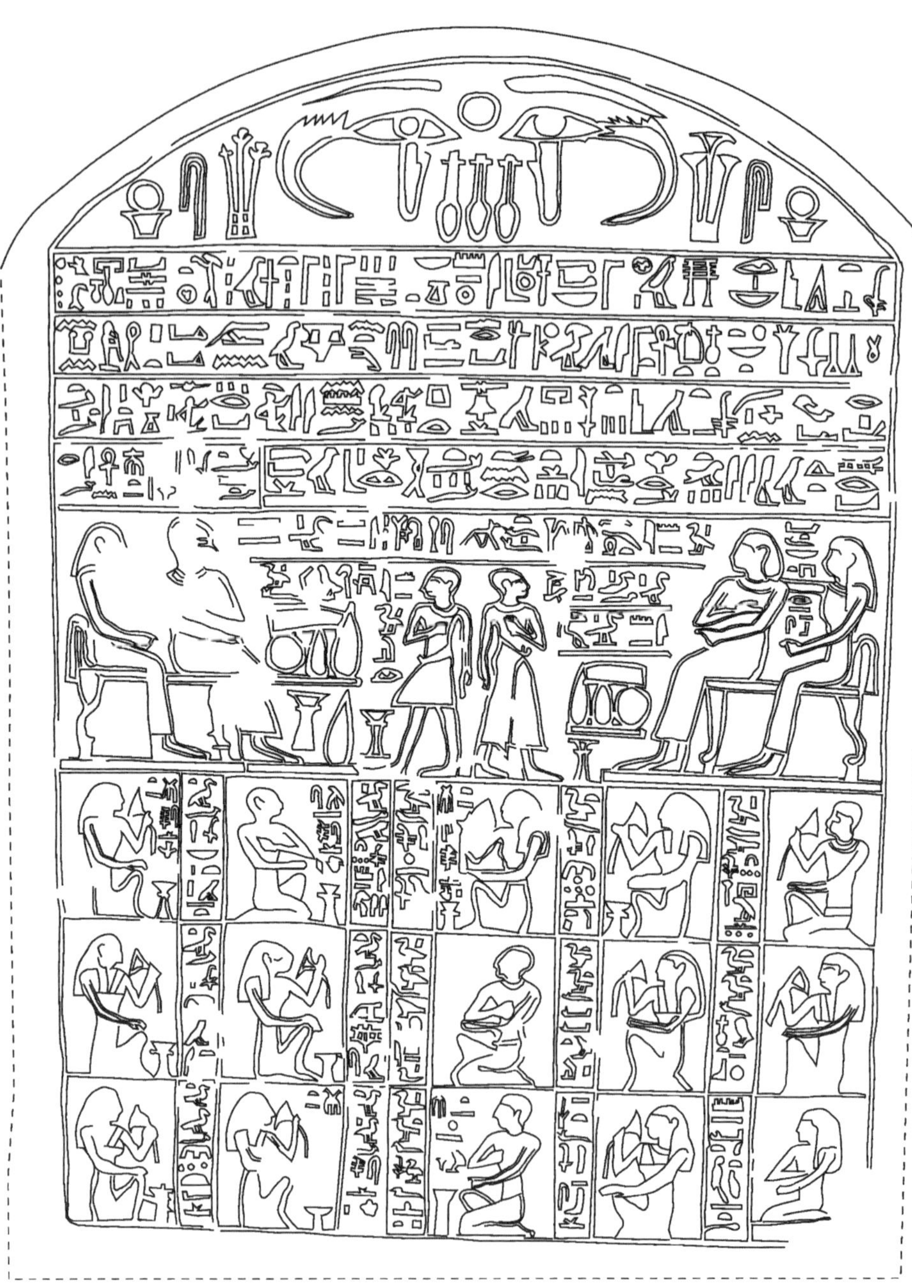

Stela, Chiddingston Castle, EDECC:01.2882 (Grajetzki, in: *IBAES* V, 61)